Fighting Inequality

Fighting Inequality

Social Justice Movements

Maria .M

Kellie D. Sikora

CONTENTS

INDEX

Chapter 1

Introduction to Social Inequality

Social imbalance is a complex and unavoidable peculiarity that has molded human social orders from the beginning of time. It incorporates a great many incongruities, including however not restricted to financial, instructive, and medical care differences. At its center, social disparity alludes to the inconsistent circulation of assets, potential open doors, and honors among people and gatherings inside a general public. This acquaintance points with investigate the different elements of social disparity, its authentic roots, and its suggestions for people and social orders.

One of the vital parts of social imbalance is monetary disparity, which appears in the inconsistent dispersion of abundance and pay. Financial inconsistencies can be seen at both the worldwide and public levels, with specific locales and nations encountering outrageous neediness while others appreciate exceptional prosperity. Inside social orders, people frequently end up situated along a range of financial honor or detriment. Factors like social class, occupation, and admittance to instructive open doors contribute essentially to one's monetary status.

By and large, monetary disparity has been propagated through frameworks of force and honor. Primitive social orders, for instance, were portrayed by an unbending class structure where the gentry held immense riches and land, while laborers worked in neediness. The Modern Insurgency achieved huge financial changes, yet it likewise prompted the rise of another class split between the modern bourgeoisie and the regular workers. These verifiable examples have left enduring engravings on contemporary social orders, where financial differences continue and, now and again, have even increased.

Instruction is another basic field where social disparity shows. Admittance to quality instruction not set in stone by elements like financial status, race, and geographic area. In numerous social orders, minimized networks face obstructions to instructive open doors, propagating a pattern of drawback across ages. Inconsistent admittance as far as possible individual potential as well as adds to the propagation of more extensive cultural inconsistencies.

The diversity of social disparity is obvious in the ways in which various types of disservice can compound and build up one another. For instance, a person who faces financial difficulty may likewise experience hindrances to getting to quality medical services, further fueling their general disservice. This interchange of elements makes mind boggling and interconnected frameworks of disparity that require extensive and multifaceted examinations.

Medical services incongruities, frequently firmly connected to financial and instructive differences, contribute essentially to social imbalance. Admittance to medical services administrations, preventive measures, and clinical therapies shifts broadly among various gatherings. People with lower financial status might confront provokes in getting to medical services because of monetary imperatives, while minimized networks might encounter segregation inside the medical care framework, affecting the nature of care they get.

Race and nationality are strong determinants of social disparity, molding people's encounters and amazing open doors in significant ways. From the beginning of time, racial and ethnic minorities have confronted foundational segregation and rejection, prompting variations in regions like business, lodging, and law enforcement. The tradition of expansionism and bondage keeps on resounding in contemporary social orders, sustaining racial progressive systems and restricting the open doors accessible to specific gatherings.

Orientation is one more basic component of social disparity, affecting people's encounters and open doors from birth to advanced age. Ladies have generally been underestimated in different circles of life, confronting separation in work, schooling, and political cooperation. The orientation pay hole stays a diligent issue, featuring the financial variations among people. Also, cultural assumptions and generalizations frequently compel people in view of their orientation, restricting their opportunity and potential.

The computerized partition has arisen as a cutting edge sign of social imbalance, as admittance to innovation and the web turns out to be progressively fundamental for cooperation in contemporary society. People without admittance to computerized assets might confront restrictions in training, business, and metro commitment. This gap can compound existing disparities, as those with computerized admittance partake in a scope of chances inaccessible to those on some unacceptable side of the gap.

The outcomes of social imbalance stretch out past individual encounters to affect the general dependability and attachment of social orders. Elevated degrees of disparity can prompt social distress, political precariousness, and a breakdown of confidence in organizations. The variations in admittance to assets and open doors make a feeling of bad form and estrangement, energizing strains between various gatherings. Tending to social imbalance isn't just an issue of equity and value yet additionally a vital stage toward building stronger and firm social orders.

Endeavors to address social imbalance require a complex methodology that tends to its underlying drivers and indications across different spaces. Strategies pointed toward diminishing financial disparity, for example, moderate tax collection and social government assistance programs, can assume a significant part in making a more fair dissemination of assets. Instructive changes that focus on equivalent admittance to quality schooling for all people, no matter what their experience, can assist with breaking the pattern of intergenerational weakness.

Advancing variety and consideration in all circles of society is fundamental for destroying the designs that propagate racial and orientation based disparities. This includes testing biased works on, encouraging a culture of inclusivity, and effectively attempting to destroy foundational obstructions. Furthermore, addressing medical care variations requires a pledge to guaranteeing widespread admittance to quality medical services administrations, paying little heed to financial status or different elements.

Worldwide collaboration is fundamental in tending to worldwide differences and advancing a more impartial conveyance of assets on a worldwide scale. This incorporates resolving issues, for example, fair exchange rehearses, obligation help for agricultural nations, and cooperative endeavors to handle issues like environmental change that lopsidedly influence the most weak populaces.

People likewise assume an essential part in tending to social disparity through grassroots developments, backing, and cognizant shopper decisions. Bringing issues to light about the main drivers and results of imbalance can add to cultural changes in mentalities and values. By testing generalizations, predispositions, and oppressive practices, people can add to the formation of additional comprehensive and just social orders.

All in all, social imbalance is a perplexing and unavoidable peculiarity that envelops financial, instructive, medical care, racial, ethnic, orientation, and computerized variations. Its underlying foundations are profoundly implanted in authentic and fundamental designs that have molded human social orders after some time. Tending to social imbalance requires an extensive and diverse methodology that thinks about the interconnected idea of various types of inconvenience.

Endeavors to battle social imbalance ought to zero in on arrangement changes, instructive drives, and the advancement of variety and consideration. Worldwide collaboration is vital for tending to worldwide abberations, while people can contribute through grassroots developments, backing, and cognizant decisions. By tending to social imbalance at its underlying foundations and cultivating a more impartial dispersion of assets and open doors, social orders can move towards more prominent equity, union, and maintainability.

1.1 Defining Inequality and Its Forms

Imbalance is an unavoidable and complex cultural peculiarity that appears in different structures, influencing people and networks across the globe. A multi-layered idea envelops variations in assets, open doors, and honors among various gatherings. To comprehend the nature and effect of imbalance, it is fundamental to investigate its definitions, basic causes, and the assorted structures it takes in various spaces of human existence.

Characterizing Disparity:

At its center, disparity alludes to the inconsistent dispersion of assets, valuable open doors, and advantages inside a general public or between social orders. This difference can appear in monetary, social, political, and social aspects, making orders and power uneven characters. Disparity is certainly not a solitary idea; rather, it is a snare of interconnected and frequently building up designs that shape people's encounters and life results.

Monetary imbalance is one of the most noticeable and broadly concentrated on types of disparity. It relates to the inconsistent dispersion of riches and pay among people and gatherings inside a general public. Abundance imbalance, frequently estimated by the circulation of resources and property, mirrors the convergence of assets in the possession of a couple. Pay imbalance, then again, measures the lopsided circulation of profit among people and families.

Social imbalance reaches out past monetary elements to envelop abberations in societal position, schooling, and medical services. Social class, race, nationality, orientation, and other personality markers add to the separation of society, deciding people's admittance to open doors and assets. This type of imbalance is well established in verifiable and primary elements, sustaining benefits for some and detriments for other people.

Political disparity appears in the inconsistent conveyance of force and impact inside a general public. It connects with people's capacity to take part in political cycles, impact direction, and appreciate equivalent assurance under the law. Political frameworks that minimize specific gatherings, confine urban cooperation, or propagate prejudicial strategies add to the steadiness of political imbalance.

Social imbalance alludes to variations in the acknowledgment and approval of various social personalities and articulations. Prevailing societies frequently direct standards, values, and portrayals, minimizing minority societies and building up power uneven characters. Media, training, and language assume huge parts in forming social accounts, affecting how various gatherings are seen and treated inside society.

Types of Disparity:

Monetary Imbalance:

Abundance Imbalance: The centralization of resources and property among a little level of the populace prompts variations in riches. This can result from verifiable variables, legacy designs, and inconsistent admittance to monetary open doors.

Pay Disparity: Inconsistent circulation of income among people and families is a typical indication of financial imbalance. Factors like instruction, occupation, and fundamental inclinations add to pay variations.

Social Imbalance:

Class Imbalance: Social class is a huge determinant of admittance to assets and open doors. Orders in light of monetary status add to the propagation of benefits and hindrances across ages.

Racial and Ethnic Imbalance: Segregation and authentic shameful acts add to abberations in open doors, schooling, work, and medical care among various racial and ethnic gatherings.

Orientation Disparity: The inconsistent treatment of people in light of their orientation is an unavoidable type of social imbalance. This appears in different circles, including the working environment, schooling, and familial jobs.

Political Imbalance:

Citizen Concealment: Limitations on casting a ballot rights and inconsistent admittance to political support add to political disparity. Minimized gatherings might confront boundaries like elector ID regulations and manipulating.

Portrayal Variations: Underrepresentation of specific gatherings in political workplaces and dynamic bodies supports power lopsided characteristics. This absence of portrayal can bring about strategies that disregard the necessities of minimized networks.

Social Imbalance:

Social Apportionment: Predominant societies appropriating components of underestimated societies without understanding or regarding their importance propagates social disparity. This frequently prompts the deletion of minority voices.

Language Authority: The predominance of a specific language underestimates speakers of minority dialects. This can restrict admittance to instruction, business, and city cooperation for people whose essential language isn't the prevailing one.

Instructive Imbalance:

Access Variations: Inconsistent admittance to quality training propagates social and financial inconsistencies. Factors like financial status, geographic area, and biased strategies add to instructive disparity.

Asset Variations: Contrasts in financing, educator quality, and instructive framework make abberations in the nature of training accessible to various networks. This adds to inconsistent results in scholarly accomplishment.

Medical services Imbalance:

Admittance to Medical care: Abberations in admittance to medical services administrations add to wellbeing disparities. Factors like financial status, geographic area, and foundational predispositions influence people's capacity to get opportune and quality clinical consideration.

Wellbeing Results: Social determinants of wellbeing, including pay, training, and work, add to varieties in wellbeing results. Underestimated bunches frequently face higher paces of bleakness and mortality.

Advanced Imbalance:

Access Differences: The computerized partition reflects imbalances in admittance to innovation and the web. Absence of admittance to computerized assets can restrict people's chances for training, business, and urban commitment.

Computerized Proficiency Holes: Contrasts in advanced education abilities add to variations in using innovation really. This can additionally minimize people who miss the mark on abilities to explore the computerized scene.

Underlying drivers of Disparity:

Understanding disparity requires an investigation of its underlying drivers, which are frequently profoundly implanted in verifiable, primary, and fundamental elements. Authentic treacheries, like colonization, subjection, and prejudicial approaches, have extensive outcomes that continue across ages. Primary variables, including financial frameworks, political organizations, and social standards, shape the appropriation of assets and amazing open doors.

1.2 Historical Roots of Social Injustice

The authentic foundations of social unfairness run profound, interweaving with the texture of human progress and forming the elements of force, honor, and mistreatment. To appreciate the current situation with social treachery, it is basic to dive into the verifiable starting points that have added to the inconsistent circulation of assets, open doors, and freedoms among various gatherings. Inspecting key verifiable ages and fundamental designs uncovers the complicated embroidered artwork of social shamefulness that keeps on influencing social orders across the globe.

One of the earliest types of social unfairness can be followed back to the frameworks of antiquated subjugation. The double-dealing of work through bondage was a far and wide practice in different old civilizations, including Greece, Rome, and Egypt. The subjugated people, frequently caught through triumphs or naturally introduced to bondage, confronted serious hardships of freedom and essential basic liberties. The propagation of bondage added to the foundation of progressive social designs, where a special class profited from the constrained work of others.

Feudalism, one more authentic framework with significant ramifications for social treachery, arose in middle age Europe. Medieval social orders were described by an unbending various leveled structure, where landowners held huge power and laborers worked the land in subjugation. The convergence of riches and influence in the possession of the medieval tip top brought about broad destitution and restricted open doors for up versatility among the lower classes. The primitive framework, with its intrinsic social imbalances, laid the preparation for resulting battles for equity and balance.

The time of investigation and colonization denoted a vital period in the verifiable foundations of social unfairness. European powers left on journeys of investigation, prompting the colonization of tremendous regions in Africa, Asia, and the Americas. The outcomes were decimating for native populaces, as frontier powers took advantage of assets, forced social predominance, and propagated fundamental shameful acts. The tradition of colonization is apparent in the getting through differences looked by native networks, from land freedoms to financial open doors.

Bondage and colonization met in the transoceanic slave exchange, a fierce section in mankind's set of experiences that effectively uprooted great many Africans to the Americas. The abuse of subjugated people for work in manors and mines filled the financial success of European pilgrim powers. The repercussions of this framework keep on resonating, as the relatives of oppressed Africans face persevering through difficulties in conquering authentic weaknesses, including monetary variations, fundamental bigotry, and social underestimation.

The Modern Transformation, while denoting a huge jump forward in mechanical and monetary advancement, likewise developed social treachery in new ways. The shift from agrarian economies to industrialized social orders prompted the development of another working people, frequently exposed to brutal work conditions and insignificant privileges. The convergence of abundance in the possession of modern entrepreneurs exacerbated financial imbalances, leading to social developments pushing for laborers' freedoms and the review of work treacheries.

The mid twentieth century saw the entrenchment of oppressive practices and foundational treacheries, especially as racial isolation and organized prejudice. The Jim Crow regulations in the US, politically-sanctioned racial segregation in South Africa, and comparative approaches somewhere else systematized racial orders, restricting the privileges and chances of minimized networks. The battle against racial unfairness turned into a focal topic in friendly developments, with pioneers like Martin Luther Lord Jr. what's more, Nelson Mandela pushing for social liberties and balance.

The twentieth century likewise saw the ascent of women's activist developments testing orientation based social foul play. Ladies' testimonial developments tried to tie down the option to cast a ballot, while resulting influxes of women's liberation resolved more extensive issues like regenerative freedoms, work environment segregation, and orientation based savagery. The verifiable foundations of orientation treachery can be followed to profoundly instilled man centric standards that have propagated power lopsided characteristics and confined ladies' independence and valuable open doors over the entire course of time.

The outcome of The Second Great War focused on the outrages of the Holocaust and the requirement for global endeavors to safeguard common freedoms. The Widespread Statement of Basic liberties, embraced by the Unified Countries in 1948, meant to lay out a typical norm for the security of principal privileges and opportunities for all individuals. Be that as it may, notwithstanding these respectable goals, social treachery endured, as decolonization battles, social liberties developments, and hostile to politically-sanctioned racial segregation endeavors unfurled all around the world.

The last 50% of the twentieth century saw the globalization of financial frameworks, correspondence, and culture. While globalization guaranteed expanded interconnectedness and potential open doors, it additionally strengthened social foul play in different structures. Monetary globalization prompted the abuse of work in agricultural nations, adding to sweatshop conditions and broadening financial variations. Social globalization, driven by media and innovation, brought both homogenizing impacts and social dominion, minimizing different voices and points of view.

The computerized age, introduced by the fast headway of innovation, achieved new components of social bad form. The computerized partition arose as an obvious sign of imbalance, with differences in admittance to data innovation restricting open doors for schooling, work, and city support. The centralization of force in tech monsters further added to financial and cultural uneven characters, raising worries about information security, algorithmic predisposition, and the effect of man-made brainpower on minimized networks.

In analyzing the verifiable underlying foundations of social shamefulness, it becomes clear that fundamental designs and imbued biases have sustained abberations across time and geological limits. While progress has been made in tending to explicit types of unfairness, the interconnected idea of social issues requires all encompassing methodologies that address underlying drivers and cultivate extensive cultural change.

The perseverance of social shamefulness brings up basic issues about the job of organizations, strategies, and aggregate activity in making an additional fair and evenhanded world. Developments for civil rights, enlivened by verifiable battles, keep on upholding for extraordinary change in regions like racial fairness, monetary equity, orientation value, and ecological equity. Grassroots activism, lawful changes, and global cooperation address roads for testing and destroying the verifiable traditions of treachery that persevere in contemporary social orders.

1.3 The Impact of Inequality on Individuals and Communities

Social disparity, with its different structures and authentic roots, applies significant and extensive effects on people and networks. The results of imbalance pervade different elements of human existence, influencing monetary prosperity, instructive open doors, physical and psychological well-being, social union, and generally personal satisfaction. To understand the full extent of these effects, it is fundamental to investigate how disparity works as a strong power molding the lived encounters of people and the aggregate elements of networks.

Monetary Effects:

At the core of social imbalance lies monetary difference, where people and gatherings experience inconsistent admittance to assets, open doors, and abundance. Monetary imbalance adds to a defined society where certain fragments appreciate benefits while others face fundamental hindrances. The effects on people are distinct, affecting their monetary solidness, work possibilities, and generally speaking financial portability.

People from underestimated bunches frequently experience impediments in getting to quality schooling and work open doors. Restricted admittance to training sustains the pattern of neediness, as people face difficulties in obtaining the abilities and capabilities fundamental for more lucrative positions. Segregation in the working environment further compounds monetary abberations, as minimized people might be exposed to bring down compensation, less headway potential open doors, and inconsistent treatment.

The legacy of monetary detriment across ages is a critical outcome of disparity. People naturally introduced to neediness face a large number of difficulties, from insufficient medical services and nourishment to unsatisfactory instructive open doors. Breaking liberated from the pattern of destitution turns out to be progressively troublesome, as foundational hindrances limit admittance to assets that could work with up friendly versatility.

Networks described by elevated degrees of monetary imbalance frequently experience social discontinuity and diminished social portability. The grouping of abundance in the possession of a couple can prompt the underestimation of whole areas, with restricted admittance to fundamental administrations like medical care, training, and foundation. This financial isolation further supports existing abberations and hampers local area improvement.

Instructive Effects:

Instruction fills in as a strong determinant of individual open doors and cultural advancement. Nonetheless, social imbalance significantly impacts instructive results, making inconsistencies that impede the potential for individual and common development. Admittance to quality training is inconsistent appropriated, with underestimated networks confronting fundamental hindrances that limit their instructive fulfillment.

Imbalance in instructive open doors starts right off the bat throughout everyday life. Variations in admittance to preschool programs, instructive assets, and extracurricular exercises add to contrasts in preparation for formal tutoring. The nature of essential and optional training can differ altogether founded on elements like subsidizing, educator quality, and the financial status of the local area.

Advanced education, frequently saw as a pathway to financial portability, isn't similarly open to all. Monetary obstructions, including the increasing expense of educational cost and restricted admittance to grants, keep numerous people from chasing after postgraduate educations. This sustains the split between those with the resources to get to advanced education and the individuals who face monetary requirements, building up existing social pecking orders.

The outcomes of instructive disparity reach out past individual conditions to influence networks at large. Networks with restricted admittance to quality schooling frequently face difficulties in labor force improvement, financial development, and municipal commitment. Instructive incongruities add to a pattern of neediness and ruin the capacity of networks to break liberated from fundamental hindrances.

Wellbeing Effects:

Social disparity significantly affects physical and emotional wellness results. Abberations in admittance to medical care administrations, day to day environments, and natural variables add to fluctuating wellbeing results among various gatherings.

People from minimized networks frequently face uplifted wellbeing endangers and decreased future contrasted with their more favored partners.

Restricted admittance to medical care administrations is a basic result of social disparity. People with lower financial status might need health care coverage, making it challenging to bear the cost of fundamental clinical consideration. Inconsistent circulation of medical care assets and offices further intensifies incongruities, as underestimated networks might have restricted admittance to quality medical services administrations.

Ecological variables, frequently connected to financial status, add to wellbeing imbalances. People in lower-pay networks might be lopsidedly presented to natural dangers like contamination, unacceptable lodging, and restricted admittance to green spaces. These circumstances add to a scope of medical problems, from respiratory infections to emotional well-being issues.

The pressure of living in states of social disparity can significantly affect emotional wellness. Steady openness to monetary difficulty, segregation, and restricted open doors can prompt persistent pressure, tension, and wretchedness. The absence of admittance to emotional well-being administrations in minimized networks further mixtures these difficulties, making a pattern of psychological well-being variations.

Local area level wellbeing effects of social disparity are clear in examples of illness predominance and medical services results. Networks confronting monetary difficulty frequently experience higher paces of ongoing illnesses, diminished future, and restricted admittance to preventive medical care measures. Tending to wellbeing inconsistencies requires a thorough methodology that thinks about the social determinants of wellbeing, including financial and instructive open doors.

Social Effects:

Social disparity disintegrates the texture of social attachment and local area prosperity. The inconsistent appropriation of assets and open doors makes divisions, cultivates question, and impedes the improvement of solid social bonds. The effects reach out past individual encounters to impact the general feeling of local area and the capacity of networks to address shared difficulties.

In people group portrayed by elevated degrees of social disparity, there is much of the time an absence of social versatility. Restricted admittance to instructive and financial open doors can prompt a feeling of sadness and disappointment among people, upsetting their capacity to imagine a superior future. This absence of up versatility adds to a pattern of generational impediment inside networks.

Social disparity can prompt the underestimation and prohibition of specific gatherings inside a local area. Unfair practices, whether in light of race, orientation, or other personality markers, make obstructions to full cooperation in friendly, social, and community life. This exclusionary dynamic adds to a feeling of estrangement and the propagation of social ordered progressions.

Trust in organizations is a setback from social disparity. Networks confronting financial difficulty and foundational separation might foster a well established doubt of organizations like government, policing, school systems. This doubt can block aggregate endeavors to resolve social issues and make a feeling of separation among networks and the organizations intended to serve them.

Social disparity additionally has suggestions for wrongdoing and law enforcement. Networks with elevated degrees of financial and social disparity frequently experience higher paces of wrongdoing. Restricted monetary open doors, combined with foundational separation, can add to the commonness of crimes as people face not many choices for monetary dependability. The law enforcement framework itself might sustain disparity through prejudicial practices and over-policing of minimized networks.

Social Effects:

Social disparity, emerging from the strength of specific social standards and accounts, impacts how various gatherings are addressed and esteemed inside society. The social effects of social disparity are apparent in media portrayal, instructive educational plans, and the safeguarding of social legacy. Underestimated people group frequently get comfortable with themselves and points of view minimized or eradicated, adding to a contorted and fragmented social scene.

Media assumes a vital part in molding social stories, and social imbalance is reflected in media portrayal. Prevailing social standards frequently become the norm, propagating generalizations and restricting the perceivability of assorted voices. This absence of portrayal supports cultural predispositions and adds to the propagation of social disparity.

Instructive educational programs, formed by verifiable predispositions and foundational imbalances, frequently present a restricted and Eurocentric perspective on history and culture. The commitments of underestimated networks might be made light of or excluded, supporting that specific social viewpoints are more important or huge than others. This restricted portrayal in schooling further underestimates specific networks and propagates social disparity.

The protection of social legacy is likewise affected by friendly disparity. Networks with restricted assets and open doors might confront difficulties in saving and communicating their social customs to people in the future. The disintegration of social legacy adds to a deficiency of personality and supports the underestimation of specific networks inside the more extensive social scene.

1.4 The Role of Social Justice Movements in Addressing Inequality

Civil rights developments assume a significant part in tending to imbalance by testing foundational treacheries, supporting for strategy changes, and encouraging an aggregate familiarity with the requirement for change. These developments, frequently determined by minimized networks and their partners, plan to destroy severe designs and make a more evenhanded and comprehensive society. Looking at the verifiable setting, systems utilized, and progressing difficulties looked by civil rights developments gives knowledge into their imperative job chasing an equitable and fair world.

Authentic Setting:

The underlying foundations of civil rights developments can be followed back to different verifiable battles against abuse and separation. Developments for social liberties, ladies' privileges, LGBTQ+ freedoms, native freedoms, and laborers' privileges have molded the direction of civil rights promotion. Every one of these developments arose because of explicit types of bad form, mirroring a common obligation to testing disparity in its different signs.

The social equality development in the US during the mid-twentieth century is a paradigmatic illustration of a civil rights development that looked to destroy racial isolation and separation. Driven by figures like Martin Luther Ruler Jr., Rosa Parks, and Malcolm X, the development used peaceful fights, common insubordination, and lawful difficulties to defy regulated bigotry. The battle for social equality prompted milestone official changes as well as catalyzed a more extensive worldwide development for racial equity.

Additionally, the women's activist development battled for orientation correspondence, testing male centric standards and pushing for ladies' privileges. Floods of women's liberation resolved issues like testimonial, regenerative privileges, working environment segregation, and savagery against ladies. The LGBTQ+ freedoms development arose to get equivalent privileges for people no matter what their sexual direction or orientation character, testing cultural marks of disgrace and lawful separation.

Native freedoms developments worldwide have tried to address authentic treacheries coming from colonization, land dispossession, and social eradication. These developments advocate for acknowledgment of native power, social safeguarding, and change for verifiable wrongs. The battle for laborers' freedoms has a long history, set apart by work developments requesting fair wages, safe working circumstances, and aggregate dealing privileges.

The verifiable setting of civil rights developments mirrors a consistent work to face dug in imbalances and backer for the privileges and pride of underestimated networks. These developments play had an essential impact in molding cultural mentalities, impacting strategy changes, and motivating ensuing ages of activists.

Systems and Strategies:

Civil rights developments utilize different techniques and strategies to challenge disparity, bring issues to light, and impact fundamental change. These methodologies are dynamic, developing because of the socio-political setting and the particular idea of the treacheries being tended to. A few normal systems incorporate grassroots getting sorted out, direct activity, lawful support, and media commitment.

1. **Grassroots Getting sorted out:**

   Grassroots getting sorted out structures the underpinning of numerous civil rights developments. This approach includes assembling networks at the nearby level, engaging people to address shared concerns by and large. Grassroots associations frequently center around building local area fortitude, encouraging initiative inside underestimated gatherings, and creating systems for backing and activism.

   Grassroots developments give a stage to people straightforwardly impacted by imbalance to share their encounters, articulate their requirements, and on the whole imagine arrangements. By encouraging a feeling of local area and mutual perspective, grassroots getting sorted out makes a strong power for social change that rises above individual endeavors.

2. **Direct Activity:**

Direct activity includes noticeable and frequently fierce techniques to cause to notice treacheries and request change. Fights, walks, protests, and different types of common defiance are normal strategies utilized by civil rights developments. These activities effectively disturb the norm, draw in media consideration, and apply strain on chiefs to resolve fundamental issues.

Direct activity brings issues to light as well as fills in for of recovering organization for minimized networks. By rampaging and declaring their entitlement to be heard, activists challenge power designs and request responsibility from those in, influential places.

3. **Lawful Promotion:**

Legitimate promotion is an essential methodology that includes utilizing the overall set of laws to challenge biased regulations, look for change for treacheries, and lay out legitimate points of reference that safeguard the freedoms of minimized gatherings. Civil rights developments frequently team up with legitimate specialists and associations to seek after case, document claims, and participate in lawful missions.

Milestone legal disputes play had a critical impact in propelling civil rights goals. For instance, the U.S. High Court choice in Earthy colored v. Leading group of Training (1954) was an essential second in the social equality development, pronouncing racial isolation in government funded schools illegal. Lawful promotion fills in as a component for deciphering the standards of equity into unmistakable legitimate securities.

4. **Media Commitment:**

Media commitment is significant for molding public stories, bringing issues to light, and accumulating support for civil rights purposes. Developments use different media stages, including customary media sources, web-based entertainment, narratives, and workmanship, to intensify their messages and contact a more extensive crowd.

Web-based entertainment, specifically, has turned into an amazing asset for putting together and preparing networks. Developments can share continuous updates, interface with allies internationally, and check deception. Hashtags and viral missions frequently act as revitalizing focuses, permitting people to contribute their voices to the bigger story.

Difficulties and Reactions:

While civil rights developments have accomplished huge triumphs, they likewise face difficulties and reactions that highlight the intricacy of tending to disparity. One test includes exploring inward divisions inside developments, as varying points of view on methodologies, needs, and authority can arise. Adjusting inclusivity, responsibility, and fortitude requires progressing exchange and reflection inside developments.

Civil rights developments are frequently met with obstruction from dug in power designs and people put resources into keeping up with business as usual. This obstruction can appear as state suppression, corporate resistance, or public backfire. Developments should explore these difficulties while keeping an emphasis on their objectives and standards.

Pundits of civil rights developments might contend that they add to polarization, subvert social attachment, or focus on character legislative issues over more extensive cultural worries. Banters around the adequacy of specific strategies, for example, direct activity or blacklists, feature the different points of view inside social orders about the best method for accomplishing social change.

Besides, the co-optation of civil rights language and images for showcasing or political purposes can weaken the extraordinary capability of developments. The commodification of activism, some of the time alluded to as "woke-washing," includes companies or people taking on moderate language without authentic obligation to considerable change. This brings up issues about the earnestness of substances professing to help civil rights aims.

The Diversity of Civil rights:

Diversity, an idea presented by Kimberlé Crenshaw, perceives that people experience numerous converging types of mistreatment in view of their different social personalities. Civil rights developments progressively underscore the significance of multifacetedness, recognizing that encounters of imbalance are formed by the convergence of race, orientation, class, sexuality, handicap, and other personality markers.

A diverse methodology provokes developments to address the exceptional encounters and needs of people who explore numerous minimized characters. For instance, a person of color might confront unmistakable difficulties that contrast from those accomplished by a white lady or a person of color. Perceiving and focusing diversity upgrades the inclusivity and viability of civil rights developments.

Worldwide Effect of Civil rights Developments:

Civil rights developments have a worldwide effect, rising above public lines and cultivating fortitude among different networks confronting comparative battles. The counter politically-sanctioned racial segregation development in South Africa, drove by figures like Nelson Mandela, drew global consideration and backing, adding to the possible destroying of the bigoted politically-sanctioned racial segregation framework.

The Bedouin Spring, a progression of favorable to a majority rules government uprisings across the Center East and North Africa, represents the worldwide idea of civil rights developments. These developments, powered by calls for political change, civil rights, and financial open door, spread across different nations, testing absolutist systems and requesting more noteworthy responsibility.

Developments for ecological equity, for example, the worldwide youth-drove environment strikes propelled by Greta Thunberg, feature the interconnectedness of social and natural issues. The call for environment equity underlines that the effects of natural corruption lopsidedly influence minimized networks, especially in the Worldwide South.

The interconnectedness of civil rights developments is apparent in the fortitude communicated by activists all over the planet. Developments upholding for LGBTQ+ privileges, native freedoms, and against bigoted drives track down normal reason chasing after equity and correspondence.

Civil rights developments, secured in the standards of value, decency, and common liberties, play had a groundbreaking impact in shaping social orders and testing settled in designs of imbalance. By looking at the verifiable development, the methodologies utilized, and the continuous effect of these developments, we gain a more profound comprehension of their importance in tending to foundational treacheries.

Verifiable Advancement of Civil rights Developments:

The foundations of civil rights developments can be followed back to early battles for essential common freedoms and poise. While these developments have different starting points, they share an ongoing idea in testing severe situation and pushing for the freedoms of minimized networks.

Abolitionist Development:

The abolitionist development, which picked up speed in the eighteenth and nineteenth hundreds of years, looked to destroy the establishment of subjugation. Abolitionists contended against the dehumanizing practice of oppressing people in view of their race and stressed the inborn uniformity of every person. Figures like Frederick Douglass and Harriet Tubman assumed vital parts in the battle against subjection, and the development laid the preparation for resulting social equality battles.

Ladies' Testimonial Development:

The ladies' testimonial development arose in the late nineteenth and mid twentieth hundreds of years, pushing for ladies' more right than wrong to cast a ballot. Activists like Susan B. Anthony and Elizabeth

Cady Stanton indefatigably lobbied for testimonial, testing profoundly imbued orientation standards. The development made ready for critical lawful changes, coming full circle in the entry of the nineteenth Amendment in 1920, which allowed ladies the option to cast a ballot in the US.

Social liberties Development:

The mid-twentieth century saw the ascent of the social liberties development in the US, pointed toward destroying racial isolation and guaranteeing equivalent privileges for African Americans. Driven by figures like Martin Luther Ruler Jr., Rosa Parks, and Malcolm X, the development utilized peaceful fights, blacklists, and lawful difficulties to defy fundamental bigotry. Milestone accomplishments, including the Social liberties Demonstration of 1964 and the Democratic Freedoms Demonstration of 1965, stamped critical triumphs for the development.

Against Politically-sanctioned racial segregation Development:

The counter politically-sanctioned racial segregation development in South Africa, traversing quite a few years, tried to destroy the bigoted arrangement of politically-sanctioned racial segregation. Activists both inside South Africa and universally prepared against racial isolation, monetary disparity, and political disappointment. The development finished in the arrival of Nelson Mandela from jail in 1990 and the possible destroying of politically-sanctioned racial segregation, prompting popularity based decisions in 1994.

LGBTQ+ Freedoms Movement:*

The LGBTQ+ freedoms development picked up speed in the last 50% of the twentieth 100 years, pushing for the privileges and acknowledgment of lesbian, gay, sexually unbiased, transsexual, and eccentric people. The Stall riots in 1969 denoted a critical second, igniting a more extensive development for LGBTQ+ privileges. Throughout the resulting many years, steps were made in testing prejudicial regulations, getting marriage correspondence, and cultivating more prominent cultural acknowledgment.

Ecological Equity Development:

Arising because of natural disparities excessively influencing under-estimated networks, the natural equity development features the inter-connection of social and environmental worries. Networks of variety frequently endure the worst part of ecological contamination, dangerous waste, and environmental change influences. The development looks to address these shameful acts and advance feasible, fair ecological approaches.

Current Developments:

Contemporary civil rights developments keep on tending to a scope of issues, including police ruthlessness, movement change, monetary disparity, and medical services access. Developments like #BlackLivesMatter, ignited in light of the killing of Trayvon Martin in 2012 and picking up reestablished speed in resulting years, advocate for racial equity and a finish to foundational prejudice.

The Me Too development, beginning in 2017, has focused on issues of lewd behavior and attack, underlining the significance of tending to drive uneven characters and cultivating a culture of responsibility. Native privileges developments universally keep on pushing for acknowledgment, sway, and change for authentic shameful acts.

The continuous development of civil rights developments mirrors a persevering through obligation to testing imbalance, destroying severe designs, and encouraging an additional comprehensive and impartial world.

Procedures Utilized by Civil rights Developments:

Civil rights developments utilize a different cluster of methodologies and strategies to challenge foundational treacheries, bring issues to light, and backer for change. These techniques frequently advance because of the socio-political setting, the idea of the shameful acts being tended to, and the particular objectives of the development.

Grassroots Getting sorted out and Local area Building:

Grassroots getting sorted out structures the foundation of numerous civil rights developments. This approach includes assembling networks at the neighborhood level, engaging people to address shared concerns by and large. Grassroots developments accentuate building local area fortitude, cultivating initiative inside underestimated gatherings, and creating methodologies for promotion and activism.

Local area building makes an establishment for supported aggregate activity, permitting people to share encounters, articulate their requirements, and all in all imagine arrangements. By engaging networks to advocate for themselves, grassroots getting sorted out forms a more comprehensive and participatory development.

Direct Activity and Common Defiance:

Direct activity includes apparent and frequently fierce strategies to cause to notice treacheries and request change. Fights, walks, demonstrations, and different types of common noncompliance are normal strategies utilized by civil rights developments. These activities disturb the norm, draw in media consideration, and apply strain on leaders to resolve foundational issues.

Common rebellion, described by demonstrations of peaceful protection from crooked regulations or approaches, has verifiable roots in developments like the social liberties development drove by Martin Luther Ruler Jr. furthermore, the Indian freedom development drove by Mahatma Gandhi. Direct activity encourages a need to keep moving, preparing networks and causing to notice squeezing social issues.

Lawful Support and Prosecution:

Legitimate support includes utilizing the general set of laws to challenge prejudicial regulations, look for review for treacheries, and lay out legitimate points of reference that safeguard the freedoms of underestimated gatherings. Civil rights developments frequently team up with legitimate specialists and associations to seek after case, record claims, and take part in lawful missions.

Milestone legal disputes play had a huge impact in propelling civil rights goals. For example, Earthy colored v. Leading body of Training (1954) in the US pronounced racial isolation in government funded schools illegal, denoting a critical second in the social equality development. Legitimate backing fills in as a component for deciphering the standards of equity into unmistakable lawful securities.

Media Commitment and Correspondence:

Media commitment is pivotal for molding public accounts, bringing issues to light, and gathering support for civil rights goals. Developments use different media stages, including conventional media sources, online entertainment, narratives, and craftsmanship, to enhance their messages and contact a more extensive crowd.

Online entertainment, specifically, has turned into an amazing asset for coordinating and preparing networks. Developments can share ongoing updates, interface with allies worldwide, and balance deception. Hashtags and viral missions frequently act as mobilizing focuses, permitting people to contribute their voices to the bigger story.

Instruction and Promotion:

Instruction and promotion endeavors are integral to civil rights developments. By giving data, assets, and apparatuses for understanding foundational issues, developments try to engage people to become advocates for change. Studios, classes, and instructive missions add to building a more educated and connected with populace.

Backing includes campaigning for strategy changes, drawing in with legislators, and activating public help for administrative changes. Developments work to impact general assessment, challenge confusions, and construct alliances that can drive strategy changes at nearby, public, and worldwide levels.

Chapter 2

Civil Rights Movements

The Social liberties Development, an essential time in American history, unfurled north of a very long while and was portrayed by an energetic battle for balance and equity. Established in the unavoidable racial separation and isolation that existed in the US, especially in the Southern states, the development meant to destroy these abusive situation and secure essential common freedoms for African Americans.

The starting points of the Social liberties Development can be followed back to the Reproduction period following the Nationwide conflict, where endeavors were made to address the social and political privileges of liberated slaves. In any case, these endeavors were fleeting as the ascent of Jim Crow regulations in the late nineteenth century introduced a period of legitimized isolation, disappointment, and fundamental prejudice.

The mid-twentieth century denoted a defining moment as the African American people group, roused by the standards of equity and correspondence, started to prepare. The development picked up speed during the 1950s and 1960s, arriving at its top with milestone regulation and extraordinary social change.

One of the early starts that touched off the Social liberties Development was the High Court's choice on account of Earthy colored v. Leading body of Training in 1954. This memorable decision announced state regulations laying out independent government funded schools for highly contrasting understudies to be unlawful, testing the scandalous principle of "separate yet equivalent."

The choice, in any case, was met with opposition from a few Southern states, starting a progression of occasions that would characterize the development. In 1955, the capture of Rosa Stops, an African American lady who would not surrender her seat to a white man on a transport in Montgomery, Alabama, prompted the Montgomery Transport Blacklist. This blacklist, coordinated by a youthful Baptist serve named Martin Luther Lord Jr., denoted the rise of peaceful dissent as a useful asset for social change.

The Southern Christian Authority Gathering (SCLC), established in 1957 by Lord and different pioneers, turned into a central participant in advancing social liberties through peaceful activism. The way of thinking of peaceful opposition, roused by figures like Mahatma Gandhi, tried to uncover the unfairness of isolation while keeping a pledge to cherish and harmony.

The demonstration development, which acquired noticeable quality in 1960, saw African American understudies arranging serene fights by sitting at isolated lunch counters. This type of direct activity expected to challenge isolation in broad daylight spaces and caused to notice the intrinsic shamefulness of denying equivalent admittance to offices in view of race.

The battle for social liberties stretched out past the Southern states, with the Northern states confronting their own difficulties of racial separation and disparity. In 1963, the Walk on Washington for Occupations and Opportunity united more than 250,000 demonstrators, requesting common and financial privileges for African Americans. The feature of the occasion was Martin Luther Ruler Jr's. notable "I

Have a Fantasy" discourse, which reverberated as a strong call for racial congruity and correspondence.

Regardless of the developing energy of the Social equality Development, progress was met with furious resistance. The utilization of savagery and terrorizing by racial oppressors, frequently upheld by neighborhood specialists, was a brutal reality. The unfortunate besieging of the sixteenth Road Baptist Church in Birmingham, Alabama, in 1963, which brought about the passings of four African American young ladies, highlighted the high stakes of the battle.

The Social equality Demonstration of 1964 denoted a critical regulative triumph for the development. This milestone regulation, endorsed into regulation by President Lyndon B. Johnson, banned separation in view of race, variety, religion, sex, or public beginning. It additionally finished inconsistent use of citizen enrollment prerequisites and racial isolation in schools, the working environment, and public facilities.

The Democratic Freedoms Demonstration of 1965 followed, tending to the efficient disappointment of African American electors in the South. The demonstration dispensed with unfair democratic practices, for example, education tests and survey burdens, that had been utilized to keep African Americans from practicing their entitlement to cast a ballot. This regulation was an essential move toward guaranteeing equivalent political interest.

The Social liberties Development confronted its portion of inner divisions and outside challenges. The ascent of Dark Power, a development underscoring racial pride and self-assurance, arose as a reaction to the apparent restrictions of the peaceful methodology. Figures like Malcolm X, a charming and articulate promoter for dark strengthening, became powerful voices inside this development.

The death of noticeable pioneers, remembering Malcolm X for 1965 and Martin Luther Lord Jr. in 1968, managed huge disasters for the development. These appalling occasions, combined with the continuous battle for monetary equity, powered banters about the best procedures for accomplishing enduring change.

The tradition of the Social liberties Development stretches out a long ways past the regulative triumphs of the 1960s. It reshaped the social and social scene of the US, testing profoundly instilled biases and motivating ensuing ages to proceed with the battle for equity. Governmental policy regarding minorities in society strategies, executed to address verifiable and fundamental disparities, were an immediate result of the development's endeavors to even the odds.

The Social liberties Demonstration of 1964 and the Democratic Privileges Demonstration of 1965 made ready for a more comprehensive and evenhanded society. Nonetheless, the excursion toward genuine balance was not even close to finished. The battle went on in different structures, including the battle against lodging segregation, police fierceness, and instructive imbalances.

In the many years that followed, developments, for example, People of color Matter arose to resolve contemporary issues of racial shamefulness. The multifacetedness of these developments featured the interconnected idea of civil rights issues, stressing the requirement for a comprehensive way to deal with destroying foundational persecution.

The idea of compensations got forward momentum as a method for tending to the verifiable and continuous effect of subjection and fundamental prejudice on the African American people group. Advocates contended for arrangements that would address financial differences, give admittance to quality schooling and medical care, and address the law enforcement framework's lopsided effect on minorities.

The continuous battle for social liberties likewise focused on the significance of perceiving and praising variety. Endeavors to advance social mindfulness and inclusivity became indispensable to making a general public where people, everything being equal, could flourish. Schools and working environments progressively embraced variety and incorporation drives, recognizing the worth of alternate points of view and encounters.

In spite of the headway made, challenges persevered. Elector concealment endeavors, especially focusing on minority networks, raised worries about the disintegration of hard-battled casting a ballot rights. The law enforcement framework kept on confronting examination for its inconsistent treatment of ethnic minorities, provoking calls for far reaching change.

The year 2020 denoted a vital second in the continuous battle for social equality. The demise of George Floyd, an Individual of color, because of a Minneapolis cop started inescapable fights and reestablished calls for equity and foundational change. The People of color Matter development picked up exceptional speed, with individuals all over the planet requesting a finish to police mercilessness and racial unfairness.

The occasions of 2020 incited a reconsideration of foundations and frameworks that sustained imbalance. Calls to undermine the police and put resources into local area based arrangements built up momentum, rocking the boat and supporting for a rethinking of public security.

The battle for social liberties likewise reached out to LGBTQ+ freedoms, ladies' privileges, and the privileges of other minimized gatherings. The battle against segregation in light of sexual direction and orientation personality picked up speed, prompting milestone legitimate triumphs and expanded cultural acknowledgment.

As the US kept on wrestling with issues of racial and civil rights, the significance of training arose as a useful asset for change. Endeavors to remember different viewpoints for school educational programs and advance a more far reaching comprehension of history planned to engage people in the future to add to an all the more and fair society effectively.

The tradition of the Social equality Development fills in as a sign of the force of aggregate activity and the getting through quest for equity. While critical steps have been made, the continuous difficulties highlight the requirement for proceeded with cautiousness and activism. The Social liberties Development established the groundwork for a more comprehensive and impartial society, provoking people and organizations to face and destroy foundational unfairness in the entirety of its structures. As the battle for social liberties proceeds, the examples of the past stay a directing power chasing a future where fairness, equity, and respect are really widespread.

2.1 The Struggle for Racial Equality

The Battle for Racial Fairness in the US has been a perplexing and persevering through venture set apart by huge achievements, difficulties, and progressing difficulties. Established in a set of experiences scarred by servitude, isolation, and foundational bigotry, the battle for racial uniformity has been a focal subject in the American story. This battle has appeared in different structures, from grassroots activism to fights in court, and has made a permanent imprint on the country's social, political, and social scene.

The earliest underlying foundations of the battle for racial uniformity can be followed back to the organization of subjection, which was profoundly dug in the American South. Subjugation, an ethically indefensible framework, dehumanized large number of African Americans as well as established the groundwork for getting through racial inconsistencies. The Nationwide conflict, battled somewhere in the range of 1861 and 1865, at last prompted the cancelation of bondage with the section of the thirteenth Amendment in 1865. Be that as it may, the finish of subjugation didn't check the finish of racial abuse.

The post-Nationwide conflict time frame, known as Recreation, saw endeavors to address the social and political privileges of recently liberated slaves. The fourteenth and fifteenth Alterations, approved in 1868 and 1870, separately, meant to give equivalent assurance under the law and guarantee casting a ballot rights paying little mind to race. Regardless of these protected corrections, Southern states executed Jim Crow regulations, organizing racial isolation and disappointment.

The mid twentieth century saw the rise of social liberties associations like the Public Metropolitan Association and the NAACP (Public Relationship for the Headway of Minorities Individuals), which looked to challenge racial disparity through lawful means. The NAACP, established in 1909, turned into a main power in the battle for social equality, utilizing case to destroy unfair regulations and practices.

The Incomparable Relocation, a mass development of African Americans from the country South to metropolitan regions in the North and West somewhere in the range of 1916 and 1970, reshaped socioeconomics and added to the development of energetic African American populations in urban communities like Chicago, Detroit, and New York. This movement powered social, political, and financial changes, laying the foundation for future activism.

The 1954 High Court choice in Earthy colored v. Leading body of Training denoted a turning point in the battle for racial balance. The decision proclaimed state regulations laying out isolated government funded schools for high contrast understudies to be unlawful, testing the idea of "separate yet equivalent." This choice set up for ensuing fights in court pointed toward destroying isolation in all parts of public life.

The Montgomery Transport Blacklist, lighted by Rosa Parks' refusal to surrender her seat to a white man in 1955, exhibited the force of peaceful obstruction as a device for social change. Driven by a youthful pastor named Martin Luther Ruler Jr., the blacklist went on for north of a year and at last prompted a High Court administering pronouncing isolation on open transports to be illegal.

The Southern Christian Authority Gathering (SCLC), established in 1957 by Martin Luther Lord Jr. what's more, different pioneers, turned into a main impetus behind peaceful activism in the Social equality Development. The way of thinking of peaceful obstruction, enlivened by figures like Mahatma Gandhi, planned to uncover the bad form of isolation while advancing affection, harmony, and fairness.

The demonstration development picked up speed in the mid 1960s as African American understudies organized tranquil fights by sitting at isolated lunch counters. This immediate activity meant to challenge isolation out in the open spaces and caused to notice the inborn shamefulness of denying equivalent admittance to offices in view of race. The Understudy Peaceful Planning Council (SNCC) assumed a key part in putting together these protests.

The 1963 Walk on Washington for Occupations and Opportunity united north of 250,000 demonstrators, requesting common and financial privileges for African Americans. Martin Luther Lord Jr's. notable "I Have a Fantasy" discourse reverberated as a strong call for racial concordance and fairness, encapsulating the development.

In spite of these additions, the battle for racial fairness confronted extreme opposition. The rough concealment of quiet fights, exemplified by occasions like the Birmingham lobby and the ruthless assault on marchers on the Edmund Pettus Extension in Selma, Alabama, featured the high stakes of the battle.

The Social equality Demonstration of 1964, a milestone piece of regulation, banned separation in light of race, variety, religion, sex, or public beginning. It additionally finished inconsistent use of elector enlistment necessities and racial isolation in schools, work environments, and public facilities. This broad regulation was a demonstration of the developing force of the Social equality Development.

The Democratic Privileges Demonstration of 1965 planned to address the orderly disappointment of African American electors in the South. The demonstration disposed of unfair democratic practices, for example, education tests and survey burdens, that had been utilized to keep African Americans from practicing their entitlement to cast a ballot. This regulation was a critical stage toward guaranteeing equivalent political cooperation.

The Dark Power development, which acquired noticeable quality in the last part of the 1960s, addressed a change in the systems utilized by certain activists. Underlining racial pride and self-assurance, figures like Malcolm X became persuasive voices inside this development. While the Dark Power development separated from the peaceful way of thinking of prior activists, it mirrored the variety of approaches inside the more extensive battle for racial balance.

Sadly, the development lost two of its most noticeable pioneers to death — Malcolm X in 1965 and Martin Luther Lord Jr. in 1968. These occasions, alongside the continuous difficulties of monetary imbalance and foundational prejudice, provoked a reconsideration of the development's systems and objectives.

The tradition of the Social liberties Development reached out past the 1960s. Governmental policy regarding minorities in society arrangements, carried out to address verifiable and foundational imbalances, meant to make everything fair in schooling and business. These strategies, while disputable, were an immediate result of the development's endeavors to address the tradition of segregation.

The battle for racial correspondence confronted new difficulties in the last 50% of the twentieth 100 years and then some. The conflict on drugs, mass imprisonment, and the racial profiling of Dark people by policing major problems. Activists and associations looked to resolve these fundamental issues, supporting for improvement in law enforcement a finish to police mercilessness.

The idea of repayments got some forward movement as a method for tending to the verifiable and progressing effect of bondage and fundamental bigotry. Advocates contended for strategies that would address monetary variations, give admittance to quality schooling and medical services, and recognize the getting through impacts of separation.

In the 21st hundred years, the battle for racial balance extended to envelop issues of natural equity, LGBTQ+ privileges, and the freedoms of other minimized gatherings. The multifacetedness of these developments stressed the interconnected idea of civil rights issues, requiring a comprehensive way to deal with destroying foundational mistreatment.

The passing of George Floyd in 2020, because of a Minneapolis cop, reignited the People of color Matter development and ignited a worldwide retribution with racial shamefulness. Dissenters rampaged, requesting a finish to police ruthlessness and fundamental bigotry. The occasions of 2020 highlighted the continuous difficulties in the battle for racial balance.

Endeavors to address racial abberations in schooling, medical services, and financial open door stayed fundamental to the battle. The significance of perceiving and commending variety acquired conspicuousness, with schools and work environments progressively embracing variety and consideration drives.

While huge headway has been made in the battle for racial fairness, challenges persevere. Citizen concealment endeavors, especially focusing on minority networks, raised worries about the disintegration of hard-battled casting a ballot rights. The law enforcement framework kept on confronting investigation for its inconsistent treatment of ethnic minorities, provoking calls for extensive change.

The battle for racial balance in the US is a continuous and developing cycle. The examples of the Social liberties Development act as an aide for people in the future, underlining the force of aggregate activity, the significance of flexibility, and the getting through obligation to equity and balance. As the country wrestles with its complicated history and makes progress toward a more comprehensive future, the battle for racial uniformity stays a characterizing section in the continuous mission for a general public where all people are genuinely equivalent, no matter what their race or nationality.

2.2 Landmark Moments in Civil Rights History

Milestone crossroads in social liberties history have molded the direction of the US, stamping crucial defining moments in the continuous battle for correspondence, equity, and basic freedoms. These minutes, scratched into the country's aggregate memory, mirror the flexibility of people and networks notwithstanding separation and persecution. From lawful triumphs to grassroots developments, these achievements significantly affect the social, political, and social scene of the country.

The Liberation Declaration, gave by President Abraham Lincoln in 1863, was a basic achievement that set up for the cancelation of subjugation in the US. While the actual declaration didn't quickly free completely oppressed people, it pronounced that all slaves an in Confederate-held area were to be liberated. The thirteenth Amendment to the Constitution, sanctioned in 1865, officially nullified subjugation, denoting the finish of a dehumanizing establishment that had persevered for quite a long time.

The Recreation period that followed the Nationwide conflict saw endeavors to get the privileges of recently liberated slaves. The fourteenth Amendment, approved in 1868, truly equivalent security under the law to all residents. The fifteenth Amendment, approved in 1870, restricted the disavowal of casting a ballot rights in light of race, variety, or past state of subjugation. While these revisions were essential strides toward social equality, they were trailed by a time of reaction as Southern states carried out Jim Crow regulations, upholding racial isolation and disappointment.

The milestone High Legal dispute of Plessy v. Ferguson in 1896 managed a critical disaster for the journey for racial balance. The court's choice, which maintained the defendability of "separate however equivalent" offices for high contrast people, gave a lawful legitimization to isolation. This administering dug in prejudicial works on, permitting states to keep up with racially isolated public offices.

The ascent of social liberties associations in the mid twentieth century denoted a recharged work to challenge racial treachery through legitimate means. The Public Metropolitan Association, established in 1910, zeroed in on monetary strengthening and social portability for African Americans. The NAACP (Public Relationship for the Progression of Minorities Individuals), established in 1909, turned into a strong power in utilizing case to challenge biased regulations and practices.

The Incomparable Relocation, a mass development of African Americans from the Southern states to metropolitan regions in the North and West somewhere in the range of 1916 and 1970, achieved critical segment and social changes. This relocation established the groundwork for the development of energetic African American populations in urban communities like Chicago, Detroit, and New York, adding to the lavishness of American culture.

The 1930s and 1940s saw the rise of figures like Thurgood Marshall, who might assume a crucial part in the fights in court for social liberties. Marshall, a lawyer and later the primary African American High Court equity, was a vital planner in testing isolation through the courts. His work laid the foundation for the milestone instance of Earthy colored v. Leading body of Schooling in 1954.

The Earthy colored v. Leading body of Training choice was a turning point in social liberties history. The High Court decided consistently that state regulations laying out isolated government funded schools for highly contrasting understudies were illegal. The choice proclaimed that the idea of "separate however equivalent" had no bearing in schooling and denoted the start of the end for sanctioned isolation in the US.

Rosa Parks' refusal to surrender her seat on a transport in Montgomery, Alabama, in 1955, lighted the Montgomery Transport Blacklist. This grassroots dissent, drove by a youthful pastor named Martin Luther Lord Jr., endured north of a year and showed the force of peaceful obstruction as a device for social change. The blacklist prompted a High Court deciding that isolation on open transports was illegal.

The Southern Christian Authority Meeting (SCLC), established in 1957 by Martin Luther Ruler Jr. what's more, different pioneers, turned into a main thrust behind peaceful activism in the Social liberties Development. The way of thinking of peaceful opposition, motivated by figures like Mahatma Gandhi, meant to uncover the foul play of isolation while advancing affection, harmony, and uniformity.

The demonstration development, which picked up speed in the mid 1960s, saw African American understudies arranging quiet fights by sitting at isolated lunch counters. This type of direct activity planned to challenge isolation in broad daylight spaces and caused to notice the inborn treachery of denying equivalent admittance to offices in view of race. The Understudy Peaceful Planning Board (SNCC) assumed a vital part in coordinating these protests.

The 1963 Walk on Washington for Occupations and Opportunity united north of 250,000 demonstrators, requesting common and monetary freedoms for African Americans. Martin Luther Lord Jr's. famous "I Have a Fantasy" discourse resounded as a strong call for racial congruity and uniformity, encapsulating the development. The walk was a significant second that added to the entry of the Social liberties Demonstration of 1964.

The Social liberties Demonstration of 1964 was a milestone piece of regulation that banned separation in light of race, variety, religion, sex, or public beginning. It denoted a huge move toward destroying regulated bigotry and isolation in different parts of public life, including schools, working environments, and public facilities.

The Democratic Freedoms Demonstration of 1965 meant to address the precise disappointment of African American electors in the South. The demonstration wiped out prejudicial democratic practices, for example, proficiency tests and survey burdens, that had been utilized to keep African Americans from practicing their entitlement to cast a ballot. This regulation was a significant stage toward guaranteeing equivalent political support.

The Dark Power development, which acquired conspicuousness in the last part of the 1960s, addressed a change in the procedures utilized by certain activists. Accentuating racial pride and self-assurance, figures like Malcolm X became compelling voices inside this development. While the Dark Power development veered from the peaceful way of thinking of prior activists, it mirrored the variety of approaches inside the more extensive battle for racial fairness.

The death of conspicuous pioneers, remembering Malcolm X for 1965 and Martin Luther Lord Jr. in 1968, managed critical disasters for the Social liberties Development. These grievous occasions, combined with the continuous battle for monetary equity, incited a reconsideration of the development's techniques and objectives.

Governmental policy regarding minorities in society strategies, executed in the last part of the 1960s and 1970s, meant to address authentic and foundational imbalances by advancing equivalent open doors in schooling and work. These strategies, while disputable, were an immediate result of the development's endeavors to even the odds for minimized networks.

The battle for racial uniformity reached out past the 1960s. Issues of natural equity, LGBTQ+ freedoms, and the privileges of other minimized bunches became key to the more extensive battle for social equality.

The multifacetedness of these developments stressed the interconnected idea of civil rights issues, requiring a comprehensive way to deal with destroying foundational mistreatment.

The 1990s saw the development of basic fights in court, including the instance of Hopwood v. Texas in 1996, which tested governmental policy regarding minorities in society strategies in advanced education. While the High Court choices in these cases didn't take out governmental policy regarding minorities in society, they put constraints on its execution.

The idea of restitutions got forward movement in the late twentieth and mid 21st hundreds of years as a method for tending to the verifiable and progressing effect of subjection and foundational bigotry. Advocates contended for approaches that would address monetary inconsistencies, give admittance to quality schooling and medical services, and recognize the getting through impacts of separation.

The passing of George Floyd in 2020, because of a Minneapolis cop, reignited the People of color Matter development and ignited a worldwide retribution with racial shamefulness. Nonconformists rampaged, requesting a finish to police ruthlessness and fundamental prejudice. The occasions of 2020 highlighted the continuous difficulties in the battle for racial equity.

Endeavors to address racial abberations in schooling, medical services, and monetary open door stayed fundamental to the battle. The significance of perceiving and commending variety acquired noticeable quality, with schools and work environments progressively embracing variety and consideration drives.

While critical headway has been made in the battle for racial fairness, challenges persevere. Citizen concealment endeavors, especially focusing on minority networks, raised worries about the disintegration of hard-battled casting a ballot rights. The law enforcement framework kept on confronting investigation for its inconsistent treatment of minorities, inciting calls for thorough change.

The battle for racial uniformity in the US is a progressing and advancing cycle. The illustrations of the Social liberties Development act as an aide for people in the future, stressing the force of aggregate activity, the significance of flexibility, and the persevering through obligation to equity and fairness. As the country wrestles with its mind boggling history and makes progress toward a more comprehensive future, the battle for racial equity stays a characterizing part in the continuous mission for a general public where all people are really equivalent, no matter what their race or nationality.

2.3 Leaders and Icons of the Civil Rights Movement

The Social liberties Development in the US was pushed by the devotion and boldness of various pioneers and symbols who assumed significant parts in testing racial unfairness and supporting for balance. These people, frequently putting their lives in extreme danger and confronting colossal resistance, turned into the main impetus behind the groundbreaking changes that unfurled during the mid-twentieth 100 years.

Martin Luther Ruler Jr., maybe the most notable figure of the Social liberties Development, arose as a charming and uplifting pioneer. A Baptist serve and expressive speaker, Lord supported for peaceful obstruction as a way to accomplish social and political change. His administration in the Montgomery Transport Blacklist in 1955 denoted the start of his unmistakable quality in the development. The Southern Christian Administration Meeting (SCLC), established by Lord and different forerunners in 1957, turned into a vital association in advancing social equality through peaceful activism.

Lord's way of thinking of peaceful obstruction drew motivation from Mahatma Gandhi's standards of tranquil dissent. His obligation to cherish, equity, and fairness was clear in the renowned "I Have a Fantasy" discourse conveyed during the 1963 Walk on Washington for Occupations and Opportunity. This milestone discourse resounded internationally, catching the embodiment of the development's yearnings for a racially coordinated and agreeable society.

In spite of his relentless obligation to peacefulness, Lord confronted various difficulties, including captures and dangers to his life. His Letter from Birmingham Prison, written in 1963, persuasively shielded the procedure of peaceful opposition and underlined the direness of the battle for social liberties. Lord's initiative reached out past regulative triumphs, impacting an age and leaving a getting through inheritance.

Rosa Parks, frequently hailed as the "Mother of the Social equality Development," turned into a meaningful figure for her job in igniting the Montgomery Transport Blacklist. Leaves, a needle worker and social liberties lobbyist, wouldn't surrender her seat to a white man on a transport in Montgomery, Alabama, in 1955. Her demonstration of resistance prompted her capture, yet it likewise touched off a 381-day blacklist of the city's transport framework by the African American people group, testing isolated public transportation.

Parks' capture and the ensuing blacklist carried public thoughtfulness regarding the issue of racial isolation and set up for legitimate difficulties to prejudicial regulations. Parks' mental fortitude and nobility turned into an image of obstruction, and her activities contributed essentially to the energy of the Social liberties Development.

Malcolm X, a strong and polarizing figure, assumed a vital part in molding the development, especially during the mid 1960s. A magnetic and articulate speaker, Malcolm X upheld for dark strengthening and self-assurance. As an unmistakable individual from the Country of Islam, he enunciated a way of thinking of aggressor obstruction and dismissed the integrationist approach supported by Martin Luther Ruler Jr.

Malcolm X's talks, for example, "The Voting form or the Shot," reverberated with numerous who felt baffled with the sluggish speed of progress in the battle for social equality. He underscored the significance of political and monetary power inside the African American population and pushed for self-protection despite savagery and abuse.

Later in his life, Malcolm X went through a change subsequent to leaving the Country of Islam. He embraced a more comprehensive vision of basic liberties and worked together with other social equality pioneers. His death in 1965 cut off his developing job inside the development, however his effect on the talk encompassing race, power, and opposition kept on resounding.

Thurgood Marshall, a spearheading lawyer and the principal African American High Court equity, assumed a significant part in the fights in court that destroyed isolation. As the main direction for the NAACP, Marshall was instrumental in the milestone instance of Earthy colored v. Leading group of Training in 1954. The High Court's decision for this situation pronounced state regulations laying out isolated government funded schools for high contrast understudies to be illegal, denoting a seismic change in the battle against organized prejudice.

Marshall's key lawful splendor stretched out past Earthy colored v. Leading group of Schooling. He contended various cases under the steady gaze of the High Court, testing biased rehearses and adding to the destroying of Jim Crow regulations. Marshall's arrangement to the High Court in 1967 denoted a memorable second, representing progress in the battle for racial balance inside the most noteworthy echelons of the legal executive.

Fannie Lou Hamer, a courageous extremist and coordinator, arose as a strong voice for casting a ballot rights and political strengthening. Hamer, a tenant farmer from Mississippi, became engaged with social equality activism when she went to a SNCC (Understudy Peaceful Organizing Board) meeting in 1962. Her activism prompted severe beatings and dangers from racial oppressors, yet she stayed unfazed.

Hamer assumed a urgent part in sorting out the Mississippi Opportunity Summer in 1964, a mission zeroed in on enrolling African American citizens in the state. Her ardent discourse at the 1964 Majority rule Public Show, itemizing her encounters of savagery and segregation, carried public regard for the predicament of African Americans in the South.

Medgar Evers, a NAACP field secretary, devoted his life to the battle against isolation and elector disappointment. Evers worked eagerly to research and archive social liberties infringement in Mississippi. His endeavors to enroll African American citizens and challenge prejudicial practices made him an objective for racial oppressors.

Unfortunately, Evers was killed before his home in Jackson, Mississippi, in 1963. His demise, alongside different demonstrations of brutality against social liberties activists, highlighted the risks looked by those rocking the boat. Evers' heritage lived on in the proceeded with battle for equity and correspondence.

Daisy Bates, a writer and social liberties lobbyist, assumed a urgent part in the combination of Focal Secondary School in Little Stone, Arkansas, in 1957. As the leader of the Arkansas NAACP, Bates directed the Little Stone Nine, a gathering of African American understudies, through the most common way of integrating the beforehand all-white secondary school.

Bates confronted gigantic antagonism, including dangers to her life, as she supported the reason for school incorporation. Her job in the Little Stone Emergency featured the difficulties looked by those supporting for integration and the strength expected to stand up to profoundly dug in bigotry.

John Lewis, a noticeable forerunner in the Social liberties Development and a long-term individual from the U.S. Place of Delegates, was an unflinching promoter for peaceful obstruction. Lewis assumed a key part in putting together the 1963 Walk on Washington and was one of the "Large Six" pioneers who arranged the occasion. His obligation to peacefulness and common defiance was obvious in his contribution in the Opportunity Rides, a progression of transport ventures testing isolated highway travel.

The fierce beating Lewis persevered during the 1965 walk across the Edmund Pettus Scaffold in Selma, Alabama, known as Ridiculous Sunday, further aroused public help for the Democratic Privileges Act. Lewis' devotion to equity and equity reached out into his political vocation, where he kept on battling for social equality and civil rights until his passing in 2020.

Ella Pastry specialist, a vital figure in the Social equality Development, was an in the background coordinator and coach to numerous activists. Pastry specialist's work centered around grassroots getting sorted out and engaging nearby networks to assume responsibility for their own battles. She assumed a vital part in the development of the Southern Christian Initiative Gathering (SCLC) and later worked with the SNCC.

Dough puncher's accentuation on participatory vote based system and her faith in the force of normal individuals to impact change affected the decentralized and grassroots nature of numerous Social liberties Development drives. Her inheritance as a tutor and coordinator reached out to the up and coming age of activists.

James Rancher, a prime supporter of the Congress of Racial Fairness (Center), was a main figure in the early Social liberties Development. Rancher's obligation to peaceful direct activity was clear in Center's Opportunity Rides, a progression of transport trips testing isolation in highway travel. The Opportunity Rides, set apart by viciousness and captures, caused public to notice the obstruction against isolation.

Rancher's essential reasoning and obligation to peacefulness added to the outcome of Center's missions. His work laid the foundation for future activists and exhibited the viability of direct activity in testing biased rehearses.

Dorothy Level, a devoted social liberties and ladies' privileges lobbyist, made huge commitments to the development for racial uniformity. As the leader of the Public Board of Negro Ladies (NCNW), Level upheld for the financial strengthening and privileges of African American ladies. She assumed a key part in putting together the 1963 Walk on Washington and was an unmistakable voice in the battle for both racial and orientation uniformity.

Level's work reached out past the Social equality Development, incorporating issues like schooling, medical services, and monetary equity.

Her initiative and support made a permanent imprint on the more extensive battle for civil rights.

Bayard Rustin, a transparently gay African American dissident and boss coordinator of the 1963 Walk on Washington, assumed a significant part in molding the technique of the Social equality Development. Rustin's mastery in peaceful dissent and his hierarchical abilities were instrumental in the outcome of the walk. Notwithstanding his critical commitments, Rustin confronted segregation inside the development because of his sexual direction.

2.4 Contemporary Challenges and the Continuing Fight for Equality

The battle for correspondence and equity in the US has been a persevering through venture set apart by progress, difficulties, and continuous difficulties. While huge steps have been made since the level of the Social equality Development, contemporary society wrestles with fundamental issues that proceed to influence minimized networks excessively. Analyzing these difficulties gives understanding into the complex and advancing nature of the battle for uniformity.

One of the enduring difficulties is elector concealment, especially focusing on minority networks. Regardless of the increases made through the Democratic Privileges Demonstration of 1965, which planned to kill unfair democratic practices, there has been a resurgence of endeavors to restrict admittance to the voting form. Measures, for example, severe elector ID regulations, cleanses of citizen rolls, and decreases in early democratic hours lopsidedly influence minority citizens, making boundaries to their political support. These strategies sabotage the central standard of a majority rules government — guaranteeing that each resident has an equivalent voice in molding the eventual fate of the country.

The law enforcement framework stays a point of convergence of contemporary battles for uniformity. Racial abberations in captures, condemning, and detainment continue, reflecting profoundly imbued fundamental issues. African Americans and others of variety are lopsidedly impacted at each phase of the law enforcement process. Police fierceness, exemplified by high-profile instances of unarmed Dark people being killed by cops, has ignited far reaching fights and calls for responsibility. The People of color Matter development, conceived out of these episodes, has turned into a strong power upholding for a finish to racial profiling, police brutality, and the militarization of policing.

Mass imprisonment, a tradition of the conflict on medications and extreme on-wrongdoing strategies, has prompted the US having one of the greatest detainment rates on the planet. The effect of this framework reaches out past people to whole networks, sustaining patterns of neediness and disappointment. Endeavors to change condemning regulations, address obligatory essentials, and elevate options in contrast to imprisonment are basic parts of the continuous battle for a fair and simply law enforcement framework.

Instructive inconsistencies stay a huge obstruction to accomplishing fairness. Notwithstanding lawful triumphs like Earthy colored v. Leading group of Training, schools in the US keep on encountering racial isolation and inconsistent admittance to assets. Differences in financing, instructive open doors, and disciplinary practices add to the tenacious accomplishment hole between understudies of various racial and financial foundations. The nature of training frequently relies upon the postal division, sustaining a pattern of disparity where understudies in minimized networks face fundamental boundaries to progress.

Monetary disparity is another contemporary test that meets with race and nationality. While the Social equality Development achieved regulative changes, financial inconsistencies persevere, with networks of variety confronting higher paces of joblessness, lower wages, and restricted admittance to monetary open doors. The racial abundance hole, a result of verifiable treacheries and unfair strategies, frustrates the capacity of underestimated networks to collect riches and intergenerational success.

Lodging separation stays a major problem, with verifiable practices like redlining enduringly affecting private examples and admittance to assets. Networks of variety frequently face obstructions to homeownership, prompting isolated neighborhoods with inconsistent admittance to quality schools, medical care, and monetary open doors. Improvement, driven by metropolitan turn of events, can uproot long-term inhabitants and compound existing disparities. Endeavors to address lodging separation, advance reasonable lodging, and make comprehensive networks are basic to the battle for fairness.

Wellbeing differences, featured by the lopsided effect of the Coronavirus pandemic on networks of variety, highlight foundational issues in medical services access and results. Underlying variables, including restricted admittance to quality medical services, financial uncertainty, and ecological shameful acts, add to wellbeing imbalances. The pandemic exposed the current weaknesses looked by underestimated networks, accentuating the earnest requirement for complete medical services change and designated endeavors to address the main drivers of wellbeing variations.

LGBTQ+ freedoms address one more wilderness in the continuous battle for uniformity. While critical headway has been made, with the legitimization of same-sex marriage being a milestone accomplishment, challenges continue. Separation, viciousness, and abberations in medical services and business excessively influence LGBTQ+ people, especially the people who are ethnic minorities. Proceeded with support for thorough enemy of segregation regulations, medical services access, and comprehensive approaches is essential to accomplishing full correspondence for the LGBTQ+ people group.

The diversity of these difficulties features the interconnected idea of civil rights issues. Minimized people frequently face covering types of segregation in light of race, orientation, sexual direction, and different personalities. The battle for uniformity requires a diverse methodology that recognizes and addresses the mind boggling manners by which various types of persecution cross and compound.

Natural equity has arisen as a basic part of contemporary battles for fairness. Networks of variety, especially those with lower financial status, frequently endure the worst part of ecological contamination, environmental change effects, and absence of admittance to green spaces. This ecological prejudice propagates wellbeing inconsistencies and worsens existing disparities. Promotion for ecological equity tries to guarantee that all networks have equivalent insurance from natural dangers and equivalent admittance to the advantages of a sound climate.

The battle against foundational bigotry and imbalance has picked up restored speed directly following high-profile occurrences of police viciousness and a developing familiarity with the well established issues confronting minimized networks. The People of color Matter development, alongside other grassroots developments, has activated individuals the country over and all over the planet to request equity, responsibility, and fundamental change.

Understood inclination and fundamental bigotry inside establishments, including policing, progressing difficulties. Changes to policing works on, including disarmament, de-heightening preparation, and expanded responsibility components, are pivotal moves toward tending to the underlying drivers of police viciousness. Calls to undermine the police and redistribute assets toward local area based drives plan to make an all the more and impartial way to deal with public wellbeing.

The job of innovation in propagating and testing disparity has become progressively critical. While virtual entertainment and computerized stages have given a space to underestimated voices to be heard and treacheries to be uncovered, they likewise present difficulties like internet based badgering, reconnaissance, and the spread of falsehood. Crossing over the advanced separation, tending to algorithmic predisposition, and guaranteeing evenhanded admittance to innovation are fundamental parts of the battle for correspondence in the computerized age.

The continuous battle for correspondence requires aggregate activity, strategy changes, and a pledge to destroying foundational obstructions. Grassroots developments, local area coordinating, and backing assume significant parts in pushing for change at neighborhood, state, and public levels. Partners from different foundations uniting with underestimated networks enhance the effect of these endeavors and add to a more comprehensive and just society.

Instructive drives that advance getting it, compassion, and decisive reasoning are fundamental in testing imbued biases and predispositions. Integrating exact and comprehensive narratives into school educational plans helps encourage a more educated and compassionate populace. Destroying generalizations and advancing social skill are fundamental stages toward making a general public that embraces variety and values the nobility of every one of its individuals.

Corporate obligation and responsibility are progressively perceived as urgent components in the battle for uniformity. Organizations and associations are being called upon to address variety, value, and consideration inside their positions, as well as in their items and administrations. Straightforward employing rehearses, pay value, and the advancement of comprehensive work environment societies add to destroying foundational boundaries inside the corporate circle.

Legitimate changes and strategy changes are key in resolving fundamental issues. Regulation that tends to oppressive practices, safeguards casting a ballot rights, and advances monetary and instructive value is essential in making an all the more society. Thorough enhancement in law enforcement, endeavors to end mass imprisonment and address police offense, is fundamental in guaranteeing equivalent security under the law.

Worldwide fortitude and mindfulness assume a part in the worldwide battle for equity. Developments for equity in one area of the planet rouse and illuminate battles in different locales. Shared encounters of separation and persecution make associations that rise above borders, stressing the interconnectedness of the battle for correspondence on a worldwide scale.

As the battle for fairness and equity in the US proceeds, contemporary difficulties highlight the steady idea of foundational issues that lopsidedly influence minimized networks. From citizen concealment and racial differences in the law enforcement framework to instructive imbalances and financial abberations, the battle for balance reaches out across different aspects of society. Inspecting these difficulties gives a nuanced comprehension of the complex and developing nature of the continuous battle for equivalent freedoms.

Elector concealment stays a huge hindrance to accomplishing a genuinely delegate a majority rules system. Notwithstanding the noteworthy triumphs of the Social equality Development, endeavors to restrict admittance to the polling form endure. Severe citizen ID regulations, cleanses of elector rolls, and decreases in early democratic hours excessively influence minority networks, making boundaries to political cooperation. These strategies subvert the standards of a majority rule government as well as sustain verifiable imbalances by disappointing minority citizens.

The law enforcement framework stays a point of convergence of contemporary battles for correspondence. Racial abberations in captures, condemning, and detainment continue, reflecting profoundly imbued fundamental issues. African Americans and others of variety are lopsidedly impacted at each phase of the law enforcement process. Occurrences of police ruthlessness, exemplified by high-profile instances of unarmed Dark people being killed by cops, have started far and wide fights and calls for responsibility. The People of color Matter development, conceived out of these episodes, has turned into a strong power supporting for a finish to racial profiling, police viciousness, and the militarization of policing.

Mass imprisonment, a tradition of the conflict on medications and intense on-wrongdoing strategies, keeps on making significant and enduring impacts. The US brags one the most noteworthy detainment rates all around the world, and the effect of this framework stretches out past people to whole networks. This pattern of detainment propagates destitution and disappointment, especially in networks of variety. Endeavors to change condemning regulations, address required essentials, and elevate options in contrast to imprisonment are critical parts of the continuous battle for a fair and simply law enforcement framework.

Instructive incongruities endure as a critical boundary to accomplishing balance. Regardless of legitimate triumphs like Earthy colored v. Leading group of Training, schools in the US keep on encountering racial isolation and inconsistent admittance to assets. Differences in financing, instructive open doors, and disciplinary practices add to the relentless accomplishment hole between understudies of various racial and financial foundations. The nature of schooling frequently relies upon the postal district, propagating a pattern of imbalance where understudies in underestimated networks face fundamental boundaries to progress.

Financial imbalance is another contemporary test that meets with race and identity. While the Social equality Development achieved authoritative changes, monetary incongruities endure, with networks of variety confronting higher paces of joblessness, lower wages, and restricted admittance to financial open doors. The racial abundance hole, a result of verifiable treacheries and oppressive strategies, blocks the capacity of underestimated networks to collect riches and intergenerational success.

Lodging segregation stays a major problem, with verifiable practices like redlining enduringly affecting private examples and admittance to assets. Networks of variety frequently face hindrances to homeownership, prompting isolated neighborhoods with inconsistent admittance to quality schools, medical services, and financial open doors. Improvement, driven by metropolitan turn of events, can uproot long-lasting occupants and compound existing disparities. Endeavors to address lodging separation, advance reasonable lodging, and make comprehensive networks are essential to the battle for fairness.

Wellbeing variations, featured by the unbalanced effect of the Coronavirus pandemic on networks of variety, highlight foundational issues in medical services access and results. Primary variables, including restricted admittance to quality medical care, financial weakness, and natural shameful acts, add to wellbeing imbalances. The pandemic uncovered the current weaknesses looked by minimized networks, accentuating the critical requirement for exhaustive medical services change and designated endeavors to address the main drivers of well-being abberations.

LGBTQ+ privileges address one more outskirts in the continuous battle for fairness. While critical headway has been made, with the legitimization of same-sex marriage being a milestone accomplishment, challenges persevere. Separation, brutality, and differences in medical care and business excessively influence LGBTQ+ people, especially the people who are minorities. Proceeded with promotion for complete enemy of separation regulations, medical services access, and comprehensive arrangements is essential to accomplishing full equity for the LGBTQ+ people group.

The multifacetedness of these difficulties features the interconnected idea of civil rights issues. Underestimated people frequently face covering types of separation in view of race, orientation, sexual direction, and different characters. The battle for correspondence requires a multi-faceted methodology that recognizes and addresses the mind boggling manners by which various types of persecution meet and compound.

Natural equity has arisen as a basic part of contemporary battles for uniformity. Networks of variety, especially those with lower financial status, frequently endure the worst part of ecological contamination, environmental change effects, and absence of admittance to green spaces.

This natural prejudice sustains wellbeing variations and fuels existing disparities. Support for ecological equity looks to guarantee that all networks have equivalent insurance from natural risks and equivalent admittance to the advantages of a sound climate.

The battle against foundational prejudice and disparity has picked up recharged speed directly following high-profile occurrences of police viciousness and a developing familiarity with the well established issues confronting underestimated networks. The People of color Matter development, alongside other grassroots developments, has activated individuals the country over and all over the planet to request equity, responsibility, and foundational change.

Implied predisposition and foundational bigotry inside establishments, including policing, progressing difficulties. Changes to policing works on, including disarmament, de-heightening preparation, and expanded responsibility components, are critical stages in tending to the main drivers of police viciousness. Calls to undermine the police and redistribute assets toward local area based drives plan to make an all the more and fair way to deal with public security.

The job of innovation in propagating and testing disparity has become progressively huge. While web-based entertainment and computerized stages have given a space to minimized voices to be heard and treacheries to be uncovered, they likewise present difficulties like web-based badgering, observation, and the spread of falsehood. Crossing over the advanced gap, tending to algorithmic predisposition, and guaranteeing fair admittance to innovation are fundamental parts of the battle for correspondence in the computerized age.

The continuous battle for fairness requires aggregate activity, strategy changes, and a guarantee to destroying foundational hindrances. Grassroots developments, local area sorting out, and promotion assume vital parts in pushing for change at nearby, state, and public levels. Partners from different foundations uniting with minimized networks enhance the effect of these endeavors and add to a more comprehensive and just society.

Instructive drives that advance getting it, compassion, and decisive reasoning are fundamental in testing imbued biases and predispositions. Integrating precise and comprehensive narratives into school educational programs helps encourage a more educated and sympathetic populace. Destroying generalizations and advancing social capability are fundamental stages toward making a general public that embraces variety and values the nobility of every one of its individuals.

Corporate obligation and responsibility are progressively perceived as urgent components in the battle for balance. Organizations and associations are being called upon to address variety, value, and consideration inside their positions, as well as in their items and administrations. Straightforward recruiting rehearses, pay value, and the advancement of comprehensive work environment societies add to destroying foundational hindrances inside the corporate circle.

Legitimate changes and strategy changes are crucial in resolving foundational issues. Regulation that tends to biased rehearses, safeguards casting a ballot rights, and advances monetary and instructive value is essential in making an all the more society. Thorough enhancement in law enforcement, endeavors to end mass detainment and address police offense, is fundamental in guaranteeing equivalent assurance under the law.

Worldwide fortitude and mindfulness assume a part in the worldwide battle for correspondence. Developments for equity in one area of the planet move and illuminate battles in different locales. Shared encounters of segregation and persecution make associations that rise above borders, underscoring the interconnectedness of the battle for equity on a worldwide scale.

3

Chapter 3

Gender Equality Movements

Orientation equity developments play had a significant impact in reshaping cultural standards and testing profoundly imbued predispositions. Since the beginning of time, these developments have tried to address the fundamental segregation and inconsistent treatment looked by people in light of their orientation. While the battle for orientation balance isn't new, the power and extent of these developments have advanced over the long run, mirroring the changing elements of social orders around the world.

One of the earliest recorded occurrences of coordinated obstruction against orientation based separation can be followed back to the suffragette development of the late nineteenth and mid twentieth hundreds of years. The essential focal point of this development was to get casting a ballot rights for ladies, who were efficiently prohibited from partaking in discretionary cycles. Activists like Susan B. Anthony and Elizabeth Cady Stanton in the US, and Emmeline Pankhurst in the Unified Realm, became famous figures driving the charge for ladies' testimonial.

The suffragette development denoted a pivotal defining moment, establishing the groundwork for resulting orientation uniformity developments. The acknowledgment that lawful freedoms and cultural perspectives expected to change turned out to be progressively obvious, and the battle for equity stretched out past the voting booth. As social orders advanced, ladies started to request equivalent admittance to training, work, and different open doors that had generally been held for men.

The mid-twentieth century saw the ascent of the women's activist development, which looked to address a more extensive range of issues connected with orientation imbalance. Woman's rights, as a socio-political development, intended to destroy the man centric designs that propagated oppression ladies. Betty Friedan's earth shattering work, "The Female Persona," featured the discontent and dissatisfaction experienced by numerous ladies who felt obliged by conventional orientation jobs.

The women's activist development picked up speed during the 1960s and 1970s, as ladies all over the planet revitalized for conceptive privileges, working environment equity, and a finish to orientation based savagery. The expression "Ladies' Freedom" turned into an energizing cry, mirroring the longing for independence and equivalent remaining in the public eye. This period likewise saw the development of different women's activist hypotheses, like liberal woman's rights, extremist woman's rights, and communist women's liberation, each offering unmistakable points of view on the most proficient method to accomplish orientation correspondence.

While the women's activist development took huge steps, it confronted analysis and reaction from the individuals who saw it as a danger to customary standards. Some contended that women's liberation planned to sabotage family structures and customary qualities, making a disruptive story that continued for a really long time. Be that as it may, the development persevered, and its effect was evident, prompting legitimate changes, strategy changes, and changes in cultural mentalities.

Notwithstanding Western women's activist developments, different districts all over the planet fostered their own extraordinary ways to deal with tending to orientation disparity. In India, for instance, the ladies' development picked up speed during the 1970s and 1980s, pushing for ladies' privileges inside the setting of a perplexing social and social scene. Issues like endowment savagery, female child murder, and inconsistent admittance to schooling were key to the development's plan.

At the same time, African nations encountered their own influxes of women's activist activism, resolving issues intended for their individual settings. Ladies in Africa pushed for financial strengthening, political portrayal, and a finish to destructive practices like female genital mutilation. These different developments highlighted the diversity of orientation imbalance, perceiving that the encounters of ladies shifted in light of elements like race, class, and social foundation.

The late twentieth hundred years and mid 21st century saw a restored center around interconnection inside the more extensive orientation uniformity talk. Multifaceted woman's rights, as expressed by researchers like Kimberlé Crenshaw, stressed the interconnected idea of social classifications like race, orientation, and class. This point of view featured the requirement for a more comprehensive methodology that tended to the covering types of segregation looked by people with converging characters.

As the computerized age unfolded, innovation turned into an amazing asset for putting together and enhancing the voices of orientation uniformity advocates. Web-based entertainment stages gave a space to people to share their encounters, prepare backing, and challenge hurtful stories. Hashtags like #MeToo earned far reaching respect, empowering overcomers of inappropriate behavior and attack to approach and share their accounts. The development rose above public boundaries, starting a worldwide discussion about the commonness of orientation based brutality and the critical requirement for change.

Notwithstanding grassroots activism, worldwide associations and states started to focus on orientation balance as a key improvement objective. The Unified Countries, through drives like the Beijing Announcement and Stage for Activity, tried to address foundational obstructions to orientation equity and engage ladies around the world. The Feasible Improvement Objectives (SDGs) embraced in 2015 incorporated a particular objective (Objective 5) zeroed in on accomplishing orientation balance and enabling all ladies and young ladies.

Notwithstanding these headways, critical difficulties endure in the mission for orientation fairness. The orientation pay hole stays an unavoidable issue, with ladies reliably procuring not exactly their male partners for a similar work. Ladies keep on being underrepresented in administrative roles in both people in general and confidential areas, restricting their impact in dynamic cycles. The weight of neglected care work, excessively carried by ladies, further compounds disparities in the labor force.

One of the persevering through difficulties in the battle for orientation correspondence is the determination of orientation based brutality. Aggressive behavior at home, rape, and provocation keep on influencing a great many people around the world, featuring the requirement for far reaching lawful structures and cultural mindfulness. Endeavors to battle orientation based brutality frequently cross with more extensive drives tending to poisonous manliness and hurtful social standards that propagate animosity and control.

The LGBTQ+ privileges development, while unmistakable from the standard orientation equity developments, shares shared objectives in testing cultural assumptions and standards connected with orientation and sexuality. Advocates for LGBTQ+ freedoms have battled for acknowledgment, acknowledgment, and equivalent privileges, adding to a more comprehensive comprehension of orientation and separating twofold thoughts of manliness and womanliness.

Strict and social factors likewise assume a critical part in molding mentalities toward orientation jobs and uniformity. In certain unique circumstances, conventional convictions and practices have been utilized to legitimize victimization ladies and breaking point their office. Orientation fairness developments have, thusly, participated in exchange with strict and social organizations, trying to advance translations that embrace equity and inclusivity.

Instruction stays a basic milestone for orientation fairness, with endeavors zeroed in on disposing of orientation based hindrances to schooling and advancing equivalent open doors for young men and young ladies. The significance of testing generalizations and inclinations inside instructive educational programs has been highlighted, as these stories frequently add to the propagation of orientation standards and assumptions.

The corporate area has progressively perceived the business case for orientation variety and incorporation. Studies have shown that different groups are more creative and perform better, provoking organizations to take on approaches and practices that advance orientation uniformity in the working environment. Drives, for example, mentorship programs, adaptable work game plans, and straightforward recruiting processes expect to establish conditions where people, everything being equal, can flourish.

Lately, the discussion around orientation balance has extended to include non-twofold and orientation nonconforming people. These people, who don't recognize rigorously as male or female, face interesting difficulties connected with cultural acknowledgment, lawful acknowledgment, and admittance to medical services. Advocates for orientation variety stress the significance of recognizing and regarding a range of orientation personalities.

The job of men in the orientation fairness development has likewise acquired conspicuousness, with a developing acknowledgment that accomplishing genuine uniformity requires the dynamic support, everything being equal. MenEngage, a worldwide collusion, urges men and young men to become partners in the battle for orientation equity, testing destructive generalizations and advancing positive manliness. This comprehensive methodology means to separate the troublesome accounts that have now and again described conversations around orientation equity.

The Me Too development, which acquired far reaching consideration in 2017, denoted a turning point in the battle against lewd behavior and attack. The development, at first centered around the encounters of ladies in media outlets, immediately spread to different areas and featured the unavoidable idea of orientation based brutality. The power elements that permitted such unfortunate behavior to flourish were uncovered, prompting expanded mindfulness and calls for responsibility.

In the domain of governmental issues, the push for orientation uniformity has appeared in lobbies for expanded portrayal of ladies in chosen workplaces. Portion frameworks and governmental policy regarding minorities in society measures have been carried out in certain nations to address the authentic underrepresentation of ladies in political positions of authority. While progress has been made, challenges persevere, including settled in orientation generalizations, unfair appointive frameworks, and the requirement for social changes in political circles.

Diversity keeps on being a core value in contemporary orientation uniformity developments, underlining the interconnected idea of different types of segregation. Endeavors to address racial and financial differences converge with orientation equity drives, perceiving that people experience covering types of mistreatment. The People of color Matter development, for example, accentuates the need to address the remarkable difficulties looked by Individuals of color in the battle against racial and orientation imbalance.

The effect of environmental change likewise meets with orientation elements, as ladies frequently endure the worst part of ecological emergencies. Orientation responsive environment approaches recognize the unbalanced effect of environmental change on ladies and underscore the significance of remembering individuals for dynamic cycles connected with ecological maintainability.

As orientation correspondence developments advance, there is a developing accentuation on cultivating inclusivity and intensifying the voices of minimized networks. Native ladies, for instance, have for quite some time been at the front of ecological and civil rights developments, supporting for their freedoms and the prosperity of their networks. The worldwide local area is progressively perceiving the significance of integrating native points of view into conversations about orientation equity and natural manageability.

The Coronavirus pandemic, while presenting exceptional difficulties, has additionally exposed the current separation points of orientation imbalance. The pandemic has excessively impacted ladies, fueling prior variations in regions like business, medical care, and homegrown obligations. Lockdowns and financial slumps seriously affect ladies in weak networks, underscoring the requirement for orientation delicate reactions to emergencies.

The advanced separation has additionally featured variations in admittance to innovation, with ladies and young ladies in certain districts confronting obstructions to online training, business open doors, and social availability. Spanning this computerized orientation hole has turned into a need for guaranteeing that the advantages of mechanical headways are evenhandedly circulated.

3.1 The Feminist Movement and Its Evolution

The women's activist development, a strong and complex social and political power, has gone through a unique development throughout the long term. Pull in the mission for ladies' privileges and balance, the development has navigated different waves, each obvious by particular objectives, techniques, and difficulties. Understanding the advancement of the women's activist development requires analyzing its verifiable setting, key achievements, and the continuous battles that shape its contemporary scene.

The underlying foundations of the women's activist development can be followed back to the late nineteenth and mid twentieth hundreds of years when ladies in Western social orders started upholding for their entitlement to cast a ballot. The suffragette development, as it was known, tried to destroy the legitimate obstructions that denied ladies the principal right to take part in appointive cycles. Activists like Susan

B. Anthony and Elizabeth Cady Stanton in the US, and Emmeline Pankhurst in the Unified Realm, assumed crucial parts in this first rush of woman's rights.

The suffragettes confronted energetic resistance, experiencing cultural obstruction and, now and again, rough constraint. The battle for ladies' testimonial laid the preparation for more extensive women's activist goals, featuring the requirement for legitimate changes to destroy regulated segregation. The primary influx of women's liberation, portrayed by its emphasis on legitimate privileges, for example, casting a ballot and property possession, set up for resulting waves that would address a more extensive range of issues.

The mid-twentieth century denoted the rise of the second rush of woman's rights, a period spreading over the 1960s and 1970s. Not at all like its ancestor, the subsequent wave expected to destroy social and cultural standards that propagated orientation imbalance. Betty Friedan's persuasive work, "The Ladylike Persona," scrutinized the restricted jobs doled out to ladies in post-The Second Great War America, igniting a cognizance raising development among ladies who felt bound by conventional orientation jobs.

The second rush of women's liberation embraced a more extremist and sweeping plan, resolving issues like conceptive freedoms, working environment segregation, and aggressive behavior at home. The individual became political as ladies tried to challenge profoundly imbued convictions about orientation jobs and declare their independence in both public and confidential circles. This wave likewise saw the development of different women's activist hypotheses, each offering particular points of view on the underlying drivers of orientation disparity.

Liberal woman's rights pushed for lawful and strategy changes to guarantee equivalent privileges for ladies inside existing cultural designs. Extremist women's liberation, then again, looked to destroy male centric frameworks completely, seeing them as intrinsically severe.

Communist woman's rights incorporated communist standards into women's activist investigation, underscoring the diversity of class and orientation battles. These different viewpoints added to a rich and nuanced talk inside the women's activist development.

While the second influx of woman's rights took huge steps, it confronted analysis and reaction from the individuals who saw it as a danger to customary qualities and family structures. The development likewise wrestled with issues of diversity, as the encounters of ladies of variety, LGBTQ+ people, and those from various financial foundations were frequently underestimated inside standard women's activist talk.

The third rush of women's liberation arose in the late twentieth 100 years and went on into the 21st hundred years, answering the apparent impediments and evaluates of the subsequent wave. This wave embraced a more comprehensive methodology, perceiving and tending to the interconnection of different types of persecution. The expression "diversity," begat by Kimberlé Crenshaw, turned into a focal idea, recognizing that ladies' encounters of segregation were formed by the convergence of elements like race, class, and sexual direction.

The third wave likewise saw the fuse of postcolonial and eccentric points of view, extending the women's activist development's extension to incorporate a more extensive scope of characters and concerns. It underscored individual organization, dismissing prescriptive ideas of woman's rights and perceiving that ladies could characterize and seek after their freedom in assorted ways. This wave saw a more prominent hug of mainstream society, innovation, and web-based entertainment as instruments for activism and cognizance raising.

One outstanding part of the third wave was its commitment with the difficulties presented by globalization. Women's activists tended to the effect of monetary globalization on ladies, especially those in the Worldwide South, featuring issues like work double-dealing, illegal exploitation, and the crossing point of orientation with different types of persecution. The World Gatherings on Ladies coordinated by the Unified Countries during the 1990s gave a stage to worldwide joint effort and support.

The approach of the computerized age additionally changed the women's activist development, giving new roads to correspondence, arranging, and activism. Web-based entertainment stages turned out to be incredible assets for intensifying minimized voices, bringing issues to light about women's activist issues, and assembling support. Hashtags like #MeToo got some decent forward movement, empowering over-comers of inappropriate behavior and attack to share their accounts and uncovering the inescapable idea of orientation based viciousness.

While the waves structure gives a verifiable outline, some contend that women's liberation is a progressing, developing cycle without unmistakable depictions. The ease and interconnectedness of women's activist battles challenge inflexible classification, and

contemporary activism frequently draws motivation from different waves all the while. By the by, perceiving these verifiable stages helps contextualize the difficulties confronted and accomplishments made by the women's activist development.

One of the persevering through provokes that women's liberation keeps on tending to is the tenacious orientation pay hole. In spite of progressions in ladies' schooling and labor force cooperation, a signifi-cant dissimilarity in profit among people wins universally. The intricate transaction of variables, including word related isolation, separation, and cultural assumptions, adds to this compensation hole.

Ladies' portrayal in administrative roles stays one more basic land-mark for orientation correspondence. The "discriminatory constraint" illustration highlights the imperceptible obstructions that upset ladies' climb to top positions of authority in different areas. Endeavors to break this roof include upholding for equivalent open doors, testing predispositions in employing and advancement, and encouraging work-ing environment societies that help ladies' expert headway.

Orientation based savagery, including aggressive behavior at home, rape, and badgering, stays an inescapable issue that the women's activist development keeps on defying. The #MeToo development, which picked up speed in 2017, uncovered the pervasiveness of sexual unfortunate behavior across ventures and ignited a worldwide retribution. While #MeToo enabled survivors to stand up, it likewise incited a more extensive social discussion about power elements, assent, and the requirement for foundational change.

Regenerative freedoms and equity have been fundamental to women's activist support, enveloping issues, for example, admittance to contraception, fetus removal privileges, and complete sex training. The politicization of ladies' bodies and conceptive decisions has been a long-standing wellspring of conflict, with women's activists pushing for substantial independence and the option to come to conclusions around one's regenerative wellbeing liberated from pressure or separation.

Comprehensive and impartial medical services stays a point of convergence for women's activist activism. The gendered effects of medical care strategies and the verifiable rejection of ladies from clinical examination have highlighted the requirement for a women's activist way to deal with medical care change. Advocates call for medical services frameworks that address the extraordinary necessities of different populaces, focus on ladies' wellbeing, and destroy predispositions in clinical examination and therapy.

The LGBTQ+ freedoms development, while unmistakable from standard women's liberation, shares shared objectives in testing cultural assumptions connected with orientation and sexuality. Women's activist points of view have added to eccentric hypothesis and activism, underlining the interconnectedness of battles against orientation and sexual segregation.

The acknowledgment of assorted orientation personalities and sexual directions inside women's activist talk mirrors a developing comprehension of interconnection.

The women's activist development has additionally participated in basic exchange with social and strict establishments, perceiving the job these foundations play in molding orientation standards. Women's activist scholars and researchers have investigated understandings of strict texts that insist orientation correspondence and challenge male centric translations. Multifaceted woman's rights recognizes the variety of strict and social encounters, cultivating a more comprehensive discourse that regards different conviction frameworks.

Training has been a critical field for women's activist support, with endeavors zeroed in on taking out orientation based obstructions to schooling and advancing comprehensive educational programs. Testing generalizations and predispositions inside instructive materials and cultivating a climate that energizes the quest for assorted fields of review have been fundamental to these endeavors. Women's activist instructional method means to make instructive spaces that enable understudies to look at and challenge cultural standards fundamentally.

The corporate area has progressively perceived the business case for orientation variety and consideration. Studies have exhibited that assorted groups are more creative and perform better, provoking organizations to embrace approaches and practices that advance orientation balance in the working environment. Drives, for example, mentorship programs, racial awareness coaching, and straightforward recruiting processes intend to establish conditions where people, everything being equal, can flourish.

The job of men in the women's activist development has acquired conspicuousness, underscoring that accomplishing genuine balance requires the dynamic support, everything being equal. MenEngage, a worldwide coalition, energizes men.

3.2 Achievements and Ongoing Struggles for Gender Equality

The excursion toward orientation equity has seen striking accomplishments throughout the long term, joined by diligent difficulties that highlight the continuous battle for a more impartial world. As headways in legitimate systems, cultural mentalities, and ladies' strengthening proceed, basic issues, for example, the orientation pay hole, underrepresentation in administration, orientation based savagery, and multifaceted segregation stay central focuses for promoters and activists.

One huge accomplishment chasing after orientation balance has been the foundation of legitimate systems to address segregation and advance equivalent privileges. Ladies' testimonial developments in the late nineteenth and mid twentieth hundreds of years effectively

upheld for the option to cast a ballot, prompting regulative changes that conceded ladies the discretionary establishment in different nations. The acknowledgment of ladies' political organization denoted an essential move toward destroying fundamental boundaries to orientation uniformity.

In the working environment, lawful measures have been carried out to address orientation based separation and guarantee equivalent open doors for people. Hostile to separation regulations, like the U.S. Equivalent Compensation Demonstration of 1963, expected to close the orientation pay hole by disallowing wage inconsistencies in view of orientation for considerably comparative work. Also, Title VII of the Social liberties Demonstration of 1964 in the US precludes business segregation based on sex, adding to the more extensive work to make comprehensive and evenhanded work environments.

Worldwide drives, like the Show on the End of All Types of Victimization Ladies (CEDAW), embraced by the Unified Countries in 1979, have given a system to tending to orientation based segregation universally. CEDAW requires the disposal of generalizations and biases, perceiving the interconnectedness of orientation uniformity with other common freedoms. While progress has been made in the approval of CEDAW, challenges continue making an interpretation of worldwide responsibilities into substantial activities at the public level.

Instructive accomplishments in the domain of orientation equity incorporate expanded admittance to schooling for young ladies and ladies around the world. Endeavors to kill orientation based hindrances to training have added to increasing enlistment rates and further developed proficiency among ladies. Associations and drives zeroed in on young ladies' schooling, for example, the Malala Asset, definitely stand out, upholding for the right, everything being equal, to get 12 years of free, safe, and quality training.

The expanded portrayal of ladies in advanced education and customarily male-ruled fields additionally checks progress in breaking orientation boundaries. Ladies seeking after professions in science, innovation, designing, and arithmetic (STEM) have tested generalizations and extended open doors for people in the future. Drives advancing STEM training for young ladies and ladies plan to address the authentic underrepresentation of ladies in these fields.

Political accomplishments in the domain of orientation equity remember the expanded portrayal of people for chose workplaces and positions of authority. Standard frameworks and governmental policy regarding minorities in society measures have been carried out in certain nations to address the verifiable underrepresentation of ladies in legislative issues. The idea of "minimum amount," underlining the requirement for countless ladies in dynamic situations to impact significant change, has built up momentum as a core value.

Milestone minutes, for example, the appointment of the principal lady to lead a nation, have represented progress in political strengthening. For instance, the appointment of Sirimavo Bandaranaike as the State head of Ceylon (presently Sri Lanka) in 1960 denoted a noteworthy second for ladies in governmental issues. Resulting many years have seen the ascent of additional ladies chiefs around the world, adding to the enhancement of political initiative.

In the corporate area, there has been a developing acknowledgment of the business case for orientation variety and consideration. Studies have shown that assorted groups, which remember individuals for administrative roles, add to expanded advancement and better monetary execution. Organizations all over the planet have executed approaches and practices, for example, racial awareness schooling, mentorship programs, and straightforward recruiting processes, to make comprehensive working environments that advance orientation balance.

The social and social scene has additionally seen shifts in mentalities toward orientation jobs and generalizations. The women's activist development, with its floods of activism, plays had a significant impact in testing and dismantling hurtful generalizations that propagate orientation disparity. Social articulations, including writing, film, and craftsmanship, have progressively reflected different and nuanced depictions of ladies and orientation elements, adding to a more comprehensive social story.

The affirmation and festivity of assorted orientation personalities and articulations have acquired conspicuousness, testing the double comprehension of orientation. LGBTQ+ privileges developments have converged with the more extensive battle for orientation correspondence, upholding for the freedoms and acknowledgment of people no matter what their sexual direction or orientation character. Legitimate progressions, like the decriminalization of same-sex connections and the acknowledgment of same-sex relationships, address triumphs for LGBTQ+ privileges and add to a more comprehensive society.

The coming of the #MeToo development in 2017 denoted a turning point in tending to lewd behavior and attack. The development, which picked up speed internationally, urged survivors to share their encounters and uncovered the pervasiveness of such unfortunate behavior across different businesses. #MeToo provoked a cultural retribution with power elements, assent, and the requirement for fundamental change in tending to orientation based viciousness.

While recognizing these accomplishments, it is critical to perceive that orientation correspondence stays an incomplete plan, with industrious difficulties requesting proceeded with consideration and activism. Overall, not exactly their male partners for a similar work. Word related isolation, segregation, and the undervaluation of customarily female-ruled callings add to this tireless dissimilarity.

Underrepresentation of ladies in administrative roles stays a huge test, both in the general population and confidential areas. The "unreasonable impediment" similitude typifies the undetectable boundaries that prevent ladies' rising to top influential positions. Endeavors to break this roof include testing predispositions in recruiting and advancement processes, upholding for equivalent open doors, and encouraging work environment societies that help ladies' expert headway.

Orientation based savagery, including abusive behavior at home, rape, and provocation, keeps on influencing people around the world, featuring the earnest requirement for complete lawful structures and cultural mindfulness. While developments like #MeToo stand out to the issue, making a social shift requires supported endeavors to challenge unsafe standards, advance assent instruction, and guarantee survivors approach backing and equity.

Regenerative freedoms and medical services access stay challenged issues in many areas of the planet. The politicization of ladies' bodies and conceptive decisions, combined with prohibitive regulations and restricted admittance to medical care administrations, upsets progress toward regenerative equity. Advocates keep on battling for far reaching sex training, admittance to contraception, and the option to come to independent conclusions about conceptive wellbeing.

The diversity of orientation imbalance further convolutes the difficulties looked by minimized gatherings. Ladies of variety, LGBTQ+ people, and those from various financial foundations frequently experience covering types of separation. Perceiving and tending to these meeting personalities is fundamental for making arrangements and mediations that are genuinely comprehensive and evenhanded.

The effect of the Coronavirus pandemic has exacerbated existing orientation disparities, excessively influencing ladies in different angles. The pandemic has prompted expanded providing care liabilities, financial weaknesses, and an ascent in orientation based brutality. Lockdowns and disturbances to schooling and medical services frameworks have had extreme ramifications for ladies, especially those in weak networks, featuring the interconnectedness of wellbeing, monetary, and orientation equity.

3.3 Intersectionality and the Inclusivity of Feminism

Multifacetedness, an idea previously presented by Kimberlé Crenshaw in the last part of the 1980s, has turned into a urgent structure for figuring out the perplexing and interconnected nature of social personalities and frameworks of mistreatment. Established in women's activist hypothesis, multifacetedness perceives that people experience numerous crossing types of segregation and honor in view of different parts of their personality, like race, orientation, class, sexual direction, and handicap. This focal point has generally reshaped how we approach woman's rights, accentuating the significance of inclusivity and recognizing the assorted encounters of ladies.

By and large, women's activist developments have now and again been reprimanded for their absence of multifacetedness, as early cycles prevalently fixated on the encounters of white, working class ladies. The women's activist development's underlying spotlight on lawful and political equity frequently neglected to address the extraordinary difficulties looked by ladies of variety, LGBTQ+ people, handicapped ladies, and those from various financial foundations. Interconnection arose as a basic remedial focal point, testing the idea of a one-size-fits-all woman's rights and pushing for a more nuanced and comprehensive methodology.

One of the vital commitments of multifacetedness to women's activist talk is its acknowledgment of the interconnected idea of frameworks of abuse. For instance, a lady's insight of segregation isn't exclusively molded by her orientation yet in addition impacted by variables like race, class, and sexual direction. This acknowledgment supports a more all encompassing comprehension of the different power elements at play in various settings, cultivating sympathy and fortitude across assorted women's activist battles.

Ladies of variety, who have frequently been underestimated inside standard women's activist developments, assume a focal part in diverse woman's rights. The encounters of bigotry, sexism, and other converging types of separation looked by ladies of variety require an unmistakable and nuanced investigation. Noticeable women's activists like Audre Lorde, ringer snares, and Angela Davis have been instrumental in forming diverse women's activist idea, featuring the significance of tending to both race and orientation chasing after equity.

LGBTQ+ people and their special battles for uniformity are indispensable to multifaceted women's liberation. The battle for LGBTQ+ privileges meets with women's activist objectives, as issues like marriage uniformity, work environment segregation, and medical services access influence people across the range of orientation and sexual characters. Perceiving and intensifying the voices of strange women's activists has extended the extent of women's activist activism, testing heteronormative suppositions and encouraging inclusivity.

Handicap privileges backing has additionally been intertwined with interconnected women's liberation. Incapacitated ladies face extra hindrances, including ableism, unavailability, and cultural mentalities that further compound their encounters of separation. Interconnection prompts women's activists to consider how different types of mistreatment converge and add to the minimization of debilitated people, underlining the requirement for a more open and comprehensive women's activist development.

Comprehensive women's liberation recognizes the different manners by which people insight and express their orientation personalities. Non-double, genderqueer, and orientation nonconforming people, frequently prohibited from early women's activist conversations outlined around a twofold comprehension of orientation, have found a home inside multifaceted woman's rights. This viewpoint challenges the prohibitive standards related with conventional orientation jobs and advances a more extensive and insisting vision of orientation character.

The acknowledgment of monetary incongruities as a vital feature of interconnection has expanded women's activist conversations around class. Average ladies, who might confront interesting difficulties like compensation double-dealing, absence of professional stability, and restricted admittance to instruction, have been integral to multifaceted women's activist examinations. Overcoming any issues among women's liberation and work privileges, this viewpoint underlines financial equity as a vital part of orientation equity.

In the worldwide setting, multifaceted woman's rights features the assorted battles looked by ladies in changed social and geographic settings. Native ladies, for example, experience crossing types of segregation established in provincial accounts, natural foul play, and the disintegration of customary societies. Interconnection prompts women's activists to draw in with and regard different social points of view while upholding for the privileges and independence of ladies all around the world.

The job of religion in molding orientation standards and assumptions is one more element of diverse woman's rights. Ladies from various strict foundations might confront particular difficulties connected with male centric translations of strict texts and practices. Multifacetedness urges women's activists to participate in exchange with strict organizations, perceiving that confidence and woman's rights can coincide and that ladies' office ought to be regarded inside different conviction frameworks.

While diversity has significantly enhanced women's activist hypothesis, its viable application stays a continuous test. Organizations and developments frequently battle to completely epitomize diverse standards in their arrangements and practices. The strain among inclusivity and the authentic designs of force inside women's activist spaces requires constant reflection and purposeful endeavors to destroy obstructions that sustain avoidance.

In training, consolidating a multifaceted viewpoint includes testing Eurocentric educational plans and tending to the different necessities of understudies. Interconnected women's activist instructional method accentuates the significance of perceiving and approving the lived encounters of understudies from different foundations. It requires an educational plan that reflects different voices and narratives, cultivating decisive contemplating crossing frameworks of persecution.

Inside the work environment, executing interconnected rehearses expects associations to go past a shallow obligation to variety. It includes resolving issues of pay value, advancing comprehensive recruiting rehearses, and establishing conditions that perceive and oblige the different requirements of workers. Diverse woman's rights in the working environment recognizes the converging personalities of people and endeavors to make spaces where everybody can flourish.

Media portrayal and social stories likewise assume an essential part in molding public discernments and supporting or testing generalizations. Multifaceted woman's rights calls for assorted and valid depictions of ladies in media, perceiving that ladies' encounters vary in view of converging factors. The consideration of different voices and viewpoints in narrating adds to a more exact and enabling portrayal of ladies in the entirety of their intricacy.

The general set of laws is a basic field for the use of diversity, requiring an extensive assessment of what regulations mean for people distinctively founded on crossing characters. Legitimate changes informed by a multifaceted women's activist system expect to address holes in assurance, dispose of prejudicial practices, and guarantee that the law mirrors the assorted encounters of people.

In spite of progress, challenges continue integrating multifacetedness into standard talk. A few pundits contend that the term has been weakened and on occasion misjudged, prompting its co-choice by substances that may not really embrace its extraordinary potential. Moreover, protection from diversity is experienced in spaces where recognizing honor and complicity in frameworks of abuse is awkward.

The strain between scholarly hypothesis and grassroots activism inside interconnected women's liberation additionally requires smart route. While the scholarly community has embraced diversity as a hypothetical structure, there is a continuous discussion about its openness and significance to grassroots developments. Overcoming this issue includes guaranteeing that multifaceted standards are converted into significant methodologies that reverberate with people on the ground.

The computerized age plays had an essential impact in enhancing diverse women's activist voices. Virtual entertainment stages give a space to people to share their accounts, coordinate developments, and challenge prevailing stories. Hashtags like #SayHerName cause to notice the special encounters of ladies of variety confronting police brutality, featuring the requirement for a multifaceted methodology in tending to foundational unfairness.

As diversity keeps on molding women's activist talk, its impact stretches out past customary women's activist spaces. Developments for racial equity, LGBTQ+ freedoms, handicap privileges, and natural equity progressively perceive the significance of multifacetedness in tending to the complicated exchange of different types of persecution. Joint efforts between various support bunches highlight the common objective of destroying meeting frameworks of imbalance.

3.4 Global Perspectives on Women's Rights

Worldwide viewpoints on ladies' privileges mirror the mind boggling exchange of verifiable, social, political, and financial variables that shape the encounters of ladies all over the planet. While progress has been made in propelling ladies' freedoms in numerous areas, determined difficulties, established in profoundly imbued standards and fundamental imbalances, keep on requesting consideration and deliberate endeavors for change. Inspecting the worldwide scene gives knowledge into the different battles and accomplishments that portray the battle for ladies' privileges on a global scale.

By and large, the battle for ladies' freedoms has taken different structures in various regions of the planet. The suffragette development in the late nineteenth and mid twentieth hundreds of years, basically in Western nations, tried to tie down ladies' on the whole correct to cast a ballot. Striking figures like Susan B. Anthony in the US and Emmeline Pankhurst in the Assembled Realm assumed essential parts in moving lawful boundaries to ladies' political support. The accomplishment of testimonial denoted a fundamental triumph for ladies' freedoms, making way for more extensive backing in resulting many years.

In the post-The Second Great War period, the ladies' freedom development picked up speed, testing conventional orientation jobs and pushing for legitimate changes. This flood of women's liberation resolved issues like work environment segregation, regenerative freedoms, and abusive behavior at home. While its effect was especially articulated in Western settings, its thoughts and standards resounded worldwide, adding to a more extensive familiarity with ladies' freedoms as a general concern.

The Assembled Countries, perceiving the significance of ladies' freedoms in the worldwide setting, laid out the Commission on the Situation with Ladies (CSW) in 1946. The CSW plays had a vital impact in advancing orientation fairness and ladies' strengthening through strategy proposals, support, and global participation. In 1979, the UN embraced the Show on the End of All Types of Oppression Ladies (CEDAW), a milestone settlement that frames the freedoms of ladies and calls for measures to end separation.

Notwithstanding these worldwide endeavors, the acknowledgment of ladies' freedoms shifts essentially across various districts. In a few Western nations, lawful systems and strategies have developed to address orientation based separation, giving roads to response and equity. In any case, challenges endure, for example, the orientation pay hole, underrepresentation in administrative roles, and progressing banters over conceptive freedoms.

In areas where the women's activist development picked up speed later, like pieces of Asia, Africa, and the Center East, the battle for ladies' privileges frequently meets with more extensive social and political changes.

At times, social standards and conventional practices present critical hindrances to the acknowledgment of ladies' freedoms. The intricacies of exploring custom, religion, and advancement make novel difficulties for ladies' supporters in these locales.

In the Center East, for instance, the talk on ladies' freedoms is molded by a complicated transaction of social, strict, and political variables.

While progress has been made in certain nations, for example, legitimate changes conceding ladies the option to cast a ballot and campaign for office, challenges persevere in regions like family regulation, where ladies might confront unfair practices. The hijab and other clothing standard guidelines additionally meet with banters around individual opportunities and cultural assumptions.

In numerous Asian nations, the battle for ladies' freedoms is intently attached to monetary turn of events and cultural changes. Quick industrialization has achieved shifts in orientation jobs, with additional ladies entering the labor force. Nonetheless, this change is frequently joined by difficulties like working environment separation, inconsistent compensation, and the perseverance of conventional orientation standards. The significance of resolving these issues is progressively perceived as fundamental for supportable turn of events.

Africa, with its different exhibit of societies and chronicles, presents a mind boggling scene for ladies' privileges backing. While progress has been made in legitimate systems and portrayal, challenges stay in resolving issues like female genital mutilation, youngster marriage, and admittance to schooling. Ladies in struggle zones might confront elevated weaknesses, including sexual brutality and removal, stressing the interconnectedness of ladies' privileges and more extensive harmony and security concerns.

In Latin America, the battle for ladies' privileges has been entwined with developments for civil rights and a vote based system. Issues like conceptive freedoms, brutality against ladies, and monetary imbalance have been vital to women's activist activism. The area has seen striking accomplishments, including the appointment of female heads of state and lawful changes tending to orientation based brutality. Nonetheless, the steadiness of machismo culture and underlying disparities keep on forming the scene of ladies' privileges.

The worldwide battle against illegal exploitation and present day servitude has likewise turned into a basic part of ladies' privileges backing. Ladies and young ladies are lopsidedly impacted by dealing, constrained work, and sexual double-dealing. Endeavors to battle illegal exploitation include global cooperation, lawful structures, and grassroots drives that expect to safeguard the privileges and respect of those helpless against abuse.

One of the determined difficulties in the worldwide quest for ladies' privileges is the orientation pay hole. Abberations in profit among people persevere in basically every nation, reflecting foundational issues like word related isolation, segregation, and undervaluation of ladies' work.

Connecting the orientation pay hole requires far reaching endeavors, including legitimate changes, work environment arrangements that advance value, and changing cultural mentalities toward orientation and work.

Viciousness against ladies, in its different structures, stays an unavoidable worldwide issue that requests dire consideration. Abusive behavior at home, rape, and illegal exploitation defraud endless ladies around the world. The #MeToo development, which picked up speed in the mid 21st hundred years, shed light on the pervasiveness of lewd behavior and attack across various enterprises, starting discussions about power elements and responsibility. Endeavors to battle savagery against ladies incorporate lawful changes, support administrations, and social moves that challenge instilled perspectives.

Conceptive privileges and wellbeing address one more basic field in the worldwide battle for ladies' freedoms. Admittance to contraception, protected and legitimate early termination, and complete conceptive medical services are focal parts of ladies' independence and prosperity. Notwithstanding, these freedoms are frequently challenged, with discusses formed by social, strict, and political elements. Advocates work to guarantee that ladies can settle on informed decisions about their conceptive wellbeing liberated from compulsion or separation.

The worldwide reaction to the Coronavirus pandemic has additionally highlighted the gendered aspects of emergencies. Ladies, especially those in weak networks, have been lopsidedly impacted by the pandemic's financial and social results. Lockdowns, interruptions to medical services benefits, and expanded providing care liabilities have exacerbated existing orientation imbalances, stressing the requirement for orientation delicate reactions to emergencies.

The computerized partition has likewise arisen as a component that impacts ladies' admittance to data, instruction, and financial open doors on a worldwide scale. While computerized advances offer roads for strengthening, ladies in certain areas face boundaries like restricted admittance to the web, advanced lack of education, and online badgering. Connecting the computerized orientation hole is fundamental for guaranteeing that the advantages of mechanical headways are fairly circulated.

The job of ladies in peacebuilding and compromise has earned respect in worldwide conversations on harmony and security. Ladies frequently assume vital parts in local area flexibility, compromise endeavors, and post-struggle remaking. The Unified Countries Security Chamber Goal 1325, embraced in 2000, accentuates the significance of ladies' cooperation in harmony processes and the need to address the particular effect of contention on ladies.

Natural equity and ladies' freedoms are interconnected worries that have acquired unmistakable quality in worldwide talk. Environmental change lopsidedly influences ladies, especially in emerging nations, where ladies might be more subject to regular assets for their vocations.

Ladies likewise assume fundamental parts in practical asset the executives and natural preservation. Coordinating an orientation point of view into environment strategies is critical for tending to the separated effects of ecological change on ladies and men.

Worldwide developments, for example, the Ladies' Walk and the Global Ladies' Strike have given stages to aggregate activity and fortitude on ladies' freedoms issues. Virtual entertainment has turned into a useful asset for intensifying ladies' voices, bringing issues to light, and preparing support for different women's activist causes on a worldwide scale. Hashtags, online missions, and computerized activism have worked with associations among activists around the world, cultivating a feeling of common perspective.

The job of worldwide associations and arrangements in propelling ladies' privileges couldn't possibly be more significant. The Feasible Improvement Objectives (SDGs), embraced by the Unified Countries in 2015, incorporate Objective 5, which explicitly addresses orientation balance. Accomplishing orientation fairness is perceived as a vital driver for economical improvement across all areas. The SDGs give a system to worldwide joint effort and responsibility in propelling ladies' freedoms.

While progress has certainly been made in the worldwide quest for ladies' privileges, the difficulties ahead are imposing. Propelling orientation correspondence requires destroying profoundly dug in structure.

Chapter 4

LGBTQ+ Rights Movements

The LGBTQ+ freedoms development, a strong and groundbreaking social and political power, has arisen throughout the course of recent a very long time as an aggregate work to get equivalent privileges and securities for lesbian, gay, sexually unbiased, transsexual, and eccentric people. This development, established in a rich history of opposition, activism, and local area building, has looked to challenge separation, battle disgrace, and promoter for the full consideration and acknowledgment of LGBTQ+ people in different parts of society.

The historical backdrop of the LGBTQ+ privileges development can be followed back to the mid-twentieth 100 years, set apart by urgent occasions, for example, the Stall Uprising of 1969 in New York City. The Stall Hotel, a famous gay bar, turned into the site of unconstrained fights against police strikes, filling in as an impetus for a more extensive development. The valiant obstruction at Stall ignited a freshly discovered feeling of fortitude and preparation inside the LGBTQ+ people group, leading to the cutting edge LGBTQ+ freedoms development.

In the beginning of the development, key figures like Marsha P. Johnson, Sylvia Rivera, and other transsexual ladies of variety assumed instrumental parts in upholding for LGBTQ+ privileges. Their activism established the groundwork for a development that would advance to incorporate a large number of issues, from decriminalization and hostile to separation measures to the battle for marriage uniformity and more extensive cultural acknowledgment.

One of the earliest achievements in the LGBTQ+ freedoms development was the declassification of homosexuality as a psychological problem. The American Mental Affiliation's expulsion of homosexuality from the Demonstrative and Factual Manual of Mental Problems (DSM) in 1973 denoted a critical stage toward destigmatizing same-sex fascination and testing destructive pseudoscientific legitimizations for separation.

All through the 1970s and 1980s, the LGBTQ+ freedoms development confronted huge difficulties, including the rise of the HIV/Helps plague. The pandemic excessively impacted gay and sexually open men and trans ladies, prompting boundless disgrace and segregation. The reaction to the emergency electrifies the local area to advocate for expanded clinical exploration, medical care access, and destigmatization of HIV/Helps.

The overwhelming effect of the pestilence additionally highlighted the requirement for more noteworthy perceivability and political commitment inside the LGBTQ+ people group. Dissident gatherings, for example, Misbehave (Helps Alliance to Release Power), coordinated dissents and direct activities to request government activity and challenge drug organizations to focus on examination and treatment. The Guides Remembrance Blanket, a strong and impactful image, honored the lives lost to the plague and filled in as a source of inspiration for LGBTQ+ freedoms.

The late twentieth century saw huge lawful and social advancement for the LGBTQ+ freedoms development, yet with progressing difficulties. The decriminalization of homosexuality in different nations, the consideration of sexual direction in enemy of separation regulations, and the battle against homosexuality regulations checked significant legitimate triumphs. Nonetheless, the development kept on wrestling with issues like work environment segregation, tormenting, and savagery against LGBTQ+ people.

The 21st century introduced another time of LGBTQ+ activism, portrayed by an emphasis on marriage uniformity. The push for the lawful acknowledgment of same-sex relationships picked up speed around the world, with milestone triumphs, for example, the legitimization of same-sex marriage in the Netherlands in 2001, making it the primary country to do as such. Resulting years saw a cascading type of influence, with numerous nations and U.S. states sanctioning same-sex marriage.

In 2015, the US High Court's choice in Obergefell v. Hodges sanctioned same-sex marriage from one side of the country to the other, a turning point for the LGBTQ+ privileges development. The decision certified that denying same-sex couples the option to wed disregarded the standards of equivalent security under the law. This triumph denoted a critical stage toward accomplishing lawful equality for LGBTQ+ people and families.

While the LGBTQ+ privileges development has taken astounding steps, it keeps on confronting difficulties and participate in continuous battles for correspondence. One critical area of center is the battle against transformation treatment, a hurtful and undermined practice that intends to change a person's sexual direction or orientation character. Numerous nations and U.S. states have done whatever it may take to boycott or limit the utilization of transformation treatment, perceiving its destructive effect on emotional wellness.

Transsexual privileges have turned into a focal point of the LGBTQ+ freedoms development, with activists pushing for lawful acknowledgment, medical care access, and insurance against separation. Issues, for example, orientation asserting medical services, comprehensive school arrangements, and exact ID archives have been at the cutting edge of the battle for transsexual privileges. The perceivability and promotion of transsexual people, like Laverne Cox and Janet Mock, have added to a more noteworthy comprehension of transsexual encounters.

The battle for LGBTQ+ privileges converges with more extensive civil rights developments, including those tending to racial imbalance and police viciousness. The unbalanced effect of viciousness and segregation on LGBTQ+ people of variety, especially Dark transsexual ladies, features the diversity of these battles. Activists work to address foundational bigotry, cultivate inclusivity, and enhance the voices of underestimated LGBTQ+ people group.

The perceivability of LGBTQ+ people in established press plays had a significant impact in molding public discernments and cultivating acknowledgment. TV programs, movies, and media portrayal that include assorted LGBTQ+ characters add to separating generalizations and testing heteronormative standards. LGBTQ+ famous people, from Ellen DeGeneres to Billy Watchman, have utilized their foundation to advocate for LGBTQ+ privileges and advance acknowledgment.

Virtual entertainment has arisen as an amazing asset for LGBTQ+ activism, giving a stage to promotion, local area building, and the intensification of different voices. Hashtags like #LoveIsLove, #TransRightsAreHumanRights, and #PrideMonth have moved all around the world, associating individuals and developments across borders. Online spaces act as center points for help, data sharing, and coordinating occasions, encouraging a feeling of worldwide fortitude.

The global scene for LGBTQ+ freedoms fluctuates essentially, reflecting assorted social, strict, and political settings. In certain nations, progress has been made in legitimate acknowledgment and assurance of LGBTQ+ freedoms, while in others, prejudicial regulations and cultural bias continue. In certain examples, LGBTQ+ people face abuse, savagery, or criminalization in light of their sexual direction or orientation character.

In nations where LGBTQ+ privileges are not completely perceived, activists work gallantly to challenge biased regulations, bring issues to light, and assemble strong networks. The battle for LGBTQ+ freedoms is profoundly interwoven with more extensive developments for basic liberties, a majority rules system, and civil rights. Activists in these settings frequently face critical dangers, including viciousness and lawful repercussions, highlighting the boldness and versatility of those pushing for change.

The job of global associations, like the Assembled Countries, in progressing LGBTQ+ privileges has acquired conspicuousness. Endeavors to advance LGBTQ+ privileges internationally include pushing for comprehensive arrangements, supporting grassroots associations, and denouncing denials of basic freedoms in view of sexual direction or orientation personality. The UN Free and Rise to battle, sent off in 2013, plans to bring issues to light and advance LGBTQ+ privileges around the world.

The worldwide LGBTQ+ privileges development keeps on defying major problems, remembering the criminalization of homosexuality for specific nations, the oppression of LGBTQ+ people, and the shortfall of lawful assurances. Advocates work to challenge prejudicial regulations, offer help for those confronting abuse, and elevate exchange to encourage understanding and acknowledgment.

4.1 The Fight for LGBTQ+ Rights Through History

The battle for LGBTQ+ freedoms has a rich and complex history, set apart by achievements, difficulties, and a steady quest for balance and acknowledgment. Spreading over many years, this battle has seen exceptional improvement, from the early provokes of imperceptibility and criminalization to the advanced battle for legitimate acknowledgment, against separation measures, and cultural acknowledgment. Following the advancement of the LGBTQ+ privileges development gives knowledge into the different techniques, activism, and social moves that have molded this continuous battle for equity.

The mid-twentieth century fills in as a beginning stage for understanding the foundations of the LGBTQ+ freedoms development. During this period, winning cultural mentalities saw homosexuality as degenerate or criminal, prompting inescapable segregation and oppression. The imperceptibility of LGBTQ+ people in standard talk added to a feeling of disengagement and underestimation.

The turning point throughout the entire existence of the LGBTQ+ privileges development is frequently connected with the Stall Uprising of 1969 in New York City. The Stall Motel, a well known social event place for the LGBTQ+ people group, turned into the focal point of obstruction when benefactors and activists, drove by transsexual ladies of variety like Marsha P. Johnson and Sylvia Rivera, opposed a police strike. The unconstrained and resistant reaction to police provocation denoted a defining moment, electrifying the LGBTQ+ people group and leading to another period of activism.

The fallout of Stall saw the development of LGBTQ+ backing gatherings and associations committed to battling for equivalent freedoms. The Gay Freedom Front (GLF) and the Gay Activists Union (GAA) were among the early gatherings shaped to resolve issues like decriminalization, hostile to separation regulations, and the destigmatization of homosexuality. Activists, propelled by the social liberties and hostile to war developments of the time, tried to challenge fundamental treacheries.

In 1973, the American Mental Affiliation's choice to declassify homosexuality as a psychological problem denoted a huge triumph for LGBTQ+ privileges. This crucial second added to changing cultural insights and testing the pathologization of same-sex fascination. It laid the basis for more extensive endeavors to destigmatize homosexuality and perceive LGBTQ+ people as a component of the different structure holding the system together.

The battle for LGBTQ+ freedoms picked up speed through the 1970s and 1980s, even as the local area confronted difficulties like the HIV/Helps scourge. The scourge, which lopsidedly impacted gay and sexually open men and transsexual ladies, prompted far reaching shame and segregation. The reaction to the emergency, set apart by the activism of gatherings like Misbehave (Helps Alliance to Release Power), highlighted the local area's versatility and assurance to battle for medical care access, clinical examination, and destigmatization.

The 1980s likewise saw the rise of the rainbow banner as a strong image of LGBTQ+ pride and fortitude. Planned by Gilbert Cook in 1978, the banner has turned into a notable portrayal of the variety and solidarity inside the LGBTQ+ people group. The banner's perceivability during Pride occasions and LGBTQ+ freedoms fights has made it a worldwide perceived image of the battle for correspondence.

The journey for legitimate acknowledgment and security got some momentum in the late twentieth 100 years. One milestone second was the decriminalization of homosexuality in different nations and U.S. states. The nullification of homosexuality regulations, which condemned same-sex connections, addressed a vital stage toward destroying lawful obstructions. Canada, for example, decriminalized homosexuality in 1969, trailed by the Assembled Realm in 1967 and a few U.S. states in resulting years.

Hostile to segregation gauges likewise turned into a point of convergence of LGBTQ+ freedoms support. The consideration of sexual direction in enemy of separation regulations expected to safeguard LGBTQ+ people from segregation in regions like work, lodging, and public facilities. While progress was made in certain wards, the absence of thorough legitimate securities stayed a test for LGBTQ+ people confronting separation in light of their personality.

The HIV/Helps emergency, which significantly affected the LGBTQ+ people group, escalated the requirement for political commitment and perceivability. Extremist gatherings like Misbehave arranged fights, exhibitions, and demonstrations of common insubordination to request government activity, expanded research financing, and admittance to life-saving medicines. The Guides Remembrance Blanket, a piercing and strong recognition for those lost to the pestilence, filled in as both a commemoration and a source of inspiration.

The 1990s denoted a time of uplifted perceivability for LGBTQ+ people in mainstream society. Network shows like "Will and Beauty" and "Ellen" highlighted LGBTQ+ characters, adding to more noteworthy portrayal and testing generalizations. Nonetheless, the ten years additionally saw the execution of oppressive strategies, like the U.S. military's "Don't Ask, Don't Tell" (DADT) strategy, which limited LGBTQ+ people from serving straightforwardly.

The turn of the 21st century carried new energy to the battle for LGBTQ+ freedoms, with a critical spotlight on marriage correspondence. The push for the legitimate acknowledgment of same-sex relationships got some decent momentum, with milestone triumphs, for example, the Netherlands turning into the principal country to sanction same-sex marriage in 2001. Resulting years saw a rush of lawful changes and court choices perceiving the option to wed for LGBTQ+ couples.

In 2003, the US High Court struck down homosexuality regulations in Lawrence v. Texas, a choice that certified the protection freedoms of consenting grown-ups took part in same-sex connections. This administering addressed a critical legitimate triumph, flagging a shift toward perceiving LGBTQ+ people's on the right track to take part in consensual connections unafraid of criminalization.

The battle for marriage fairness arrived at a memorable achievement in 2015 with the US High Court's choice in Obergefell v. Hodges. The decision pronounced that denying same-sex couples the option to wed abused the standards of equivalent insurance under the law. This milestone choice legitimized same-sex marriage cross country, denoting an extraordinary second in the LGBTQ+ freedoms development.

While the LGBTQ+ privileges development has celebrated huge triumphs, it keeps on confronting progressing difficulties and take part in basic battles. One such region is the battle against transformation treatment, an unsafe and defamed practice that expects to change a

person's sexual direction or orientation character. Endeavors to boycott or confine the utilization of change treatment have built up some forward movement around the world, perceiving the training's serious effect on psychological well-being.

Transsexual freedoms have turned into a focal point of the LGBTQ+ privileges development, with activists supporting for lawful acknowledgment, medical services access, and security against segregation. The battle for transsexual privileges envelops issues, for example, orientation insisting medical services, comprehensive school arrangements, and exact ID reports. The perceivability and backing of transsexual people, like Laverne Cox and Janet Mock, have added to a more prominent comprehension of transsexual encounters.

The battle for LGBTQ+ privileges crosses with more extensive civil rights developments, including those tending to racial imbalance and police brutality. The unbalanced effect of brutality and segregation on LGBTQ+ people of variety, especially Dark transsexual ladies, features the interconnection of these battles. Activists work to address fundamental bigotry, cultivate inclusivity, and enhance the voices of underestimated LGBTQ+ people group.

The perceivability of LGBTQ+ people in traditional press plays had a urgent impact in forming public discernments and cultivating acknowledgment. Network shows, movies, and media portrayal that include assorted LGBTQ+ characters add to separating generalizations and testing heteronormative standards. LGBTQ+ VIPs, from Ellen DeGeneres to Billy Watchman, have utilized their foundation to advocate for LGBTQ+ privileges and advance acknowledgment.

Online entertainment has arisen as a useful asset for LGBTQ+ activism, giving a stage to support, local area building, and the intensification of different voices. Hashtags like #LoveIsLove, #TransRightsAreHumanRights, and #PrideMonth have moved worldwide, associating individuals and developments across borders. Online spaces act as centers for help, data sharing, and coordinating occasions, cultivating a feeling of worldwide fortitude.

The worldwide scene for LGBTQ+ privileges differs essentially, reflecting different social, strict, and political settings. In certain nations, progress has been made in legitimate acknowledgment and security of LGBTQ+ privileges, while in others, oppressive regulations and cultural bias continue. In certain examples, LGBTQ+ people face mistreatment, viciousness, or criminalization in view of their sexual direction or orientation personality.

4.2 Legal Milestones and Social Acceptance

The excursion toward LGBTQ+ privileges and social acknowledgment has been significantly impacted by legitimate achievements that reflect advancing cultural perspectives. These lawful triumphs, frequently accomplished through essential suit, official changes, and support, play had a significant impact in destroying unfair practices and cultivating a more comprehensive and tolerating society. Looking at these legitimate achievements gives understanding into the perplexing transaction between the law and social change in the domain of LGBTQ+ privileges.

One of the early legitimate achievements in the LGBTQ+ privileges development was the decriminalization of homosexuality. In many areas of the planet, regulations condemning same-sex connections continued all the way into the twentieth hundred years, adding to the minimization and abuse of LGBTQ+ people. The decriminalization cycle denoted a seismic shift, recognizing the privileges of people to take part in consensual connections unafraid of lawful repercussions.

The decriminalization of homosexuality was a slow cycle that unfurled across various nations and districts. In 1967, the Unified Realm made a notable stride by decriminalizing homosexuality in Britain and Ribs. The Sexual Offenses Demonstration of 1967 legitimized consensual sex between men beyond 21 years old in private. Comparable legitimate changes happened in resulting years, with different nations returning to and revoking outdated regulations that condemned same-sex connections.

The US encountered a huge legitimate achievement with the High Court's decision in Lawrence v. Texas in 2003. This milestone choice announced homosexuality regulations illegal, toppling past decisions that had maintained state regulations condemning same-sex connections. The Lawrence choice confirmed the security freedoms of consenting grown-ups and denoted a urgent second in the acknowledgment of LGBTQ+ people's on the right track to participate in personal connections without state obstruction.

Expanding on the decriminalization endeavors, the LGBTQ+ freedoms development directed its concentration toward against separation measures. Consideration of sexual direction and orientation personality in enemy of segregation regulations turned into a critical objective, planning to safeguard LGBTQ+ people from separation in different circles of life, including work, lodging, and public facilities.

The entry of the Business Non-Segregation Act (ENDA) in the US denoted a huge move toward safeguarding LGBTQ+ people in the working environment. While the bill confronted difficulties and has not become government regulation, a few U.S. states and nearby locales have authorized their own non-separation regulations, giving lawful response to people confronting segregation in light of sexual direction or orientation personality.

Globally, the battle against separation became the dominant focal point with the foundation of the Assembled Countries (UN) Free and Rise to crusade in 2013. This worldwide drive tries to advance LGBTQ+ freedoms and bring issues to light about the effect of separation and savagery on LGBTQ+ people. Endeavors like the Free and Rise to crusade add to cultivating a worldwide discussion on the significance of legitimate securities for LGBTQ+ people.

Marriage correspondence addresses one of the most groundbreaking lawful achievements in the LGBTQ+ freedoms development. The battle for the legitimate acknowledgment of same-sex relationships picked up speed in the mid 21st 100 years, with milestone triumphs that reshaped the cultural comprehension of marriage and love.

The Netherlands turned into the primary country to legitimize same-sex marriage in 2001, starting a trend for a rush of worldwide changes. Nations like Belgium, Spain, Canada, and South Africa followed after accordingly, perceiving the right of same-sex couples to wed. These lawful triumphs reflected changing cultural mentalities and denoted a take-off from customary standards that had long barred LGBTQ+ people from the establishment of marriage.

In the US, the way to marriage correspondence included a progression of fights in court, support endeavors, and social movements. The Guard of Marriage Act (DOMA), ordered in 1996, characterized marriage at the government level as a joining between one man and one lady. This prohibitive definition was tested in the milestone case US v. Windsor in 2013, where the High Court struck down key arrangements of DOMA, making ready for government acknowledgment of same-sex relationships.

The apex of the marriage balance development in the US accompanied the High Court's choice in Obergefell v. Hodges in 2015. The decision held that denying same-sex couples the option to wed disregarded the Equivalent Insurance Provision of the Fourteenth Amendment. This noteworthy choice sanctioned same-sex marriage cross country, perceiving the principal right of LGBTQ+ people to go into the organization of marriage.

Past lawful changes, the LGBTQ+ privileges development has tried to resolve issues connected with transsexual freedoms and personality documentation. The lawful acknowledgment of orientation personality and the right to precise recognizable proof archives have become focal parts of the battle for transsexual privileges.

Argentina stands apart as a trailblazer in perceiving transsexual freedoms, especially in the domain of legitimate orientation acknowledgment. In 2012, Argentina passed the Orientation Character Regulation, permitting people to change their orientation marker on true reports without the requirement for clinical mediations or legal endorsement. This historic regulation set a model for different nations wrestling with issues of lawful acknowledgment for transsexual people.

Lawful triumphs in the space of transsexual freedoms have reached out to the work environment also. A few nations and wards have executed legitimate insurances against separation in view of orientation character and articulation. These actions add to encouraging comprehensive working environments and testing unfair practices that excessively influence transsexual people.

The battle against change treatment addresses one more basic lawful landmark in the LGBTQ+ privileges development. Transformation treatment, otherwise called reparative treatment, alludes to rehearses pointed toward changing a person's sexual direction or orientation character. Numerous clinical and psychological wellness associations have censured these practices as ineffectual, hurtful, and exploitative.

A few U.S. states and nations have done whatever it takes to boycott or confine the utilization of change treatment on minors. Lawful measures change, going from out and out boycotts to limitations on authorized advisors taking part in these practices. These legitimate mediations mirror a developing comprehension of the potential mischief brought about by change treatment and the need to shield LGBTQ+ youth from these practices.

While legitimate achievements have without a doubt pushed the LGBTQ+ freedoms progress ahead, the journey for social acknowledgment stays a continuous and nuanced challenge. Accomplishing lawful equity doesn't necessarily in every case convert into prompt cultural acknowledgment, and the LGBTQ+ people group keeps on wrestling with issues of segregation, shame, and bias.

Media portrayal plays had a vital impact in molding cultural perspectives toward the LGBTQ+ people group. Network shows, films, and different types of media that include assorted and true LGBTQ+ characters add to separating generalizations and encouraging sympathy. Expanded perceivability in the media helps challenge heteronormative standards and advances a more comprehensive comprehension of human connections and characters.

The diversity of LGBTQ+ characters with race, nationality, and different parts of individual personality adds layers of intricacy to the battle for social acknowledgment. LGBTQ+ people of variety, especially transsexual ladies of variety, frequently face converging types of segregation and brutality. Backing endeavors should address these crossing difficulties and work toward inclusivity inside the more extensive LGBTQ+ privileges development.

Social acknowledgment likewise includes encouraging LGBTQ+ inclusivity in instructive establishments. Backing for LGBTQ+ comprehensive educational programs, steady arrangements, and places of refuge inside schools adds to establishing a climate where LGBTQ+ youth can flourish. Endeavors to battle harassing, separation, and provocation are fundamental parts of making comprehensive instructive spaces.

Strict organizations have been the two destinations of obstruction and wellsprings of resistance to LGBTQ+ freedoms. The battle for social acknowledgment frequently includes drawing in with strict networks to encourage exchange, challenge biased rehearses, and advance getting it. Numerous strict pioneers and associations have embraced LGBTQ+ consideration, pushing for attesting religious philosophy and inviting gatherings.

The approach of web-based entertainment has given a stage to LGBTQ+ people and partners to interface, share stories, and fabricate networks. Online spaces add to the perceivability of different encounters inside the LGBTQ+ people group and give a steady climate to people exploring their characters. Virtual entertainment has likewise been a useful asset for sorting out and preparing backing endeavors.

Notwithstanding the headway made through lawful achievements and moving cultural mentalities, challenges continue. Disdain violations focusing on LGBTQ+ people, especially transsexual people and LGBTQ+ people of variety, stay a squeezing concern. Resolving foundational issues of savagery and separation requires a far reaching approach that consolidates lawful measures, schooling, and local area commitment.

The battle for LGBTQ+ privileges and social acknowledgment is essentially associated with the more extensive battle for basic liberties and poise. Activists, partners, and people inside the LGBTQ+ people group keep on pursuing an existence where everybody, no matter what their sexual direction or orientation personality, can reside liberated from segregation, appreciate legitimate securities, and experience certifiable social acknowledgment.

4.3 Transgender Rights and Intersectional Advocacy

The backing for transsexual privileges addresses a basic wilderness in the more extensive battle for LGBTQ+ balance. Transsexual people, whose orientation character varies from the sex doled out to them upon entering the world, face special difficulties and types of separation. The battle for transsexual freedoms incorporates legitimate acknowledgment, medical care access, assurance against separation, and cultural acknowledgment. Furthermore, the multifacetedness of transsexual characters with race, nationality, and different elements highlights the requirement for comprehensive and interconnected promotion that tends to the assorted encounters inside the transsexual local area.

One of the primary parts of transsexual privileges promotion is lawful acknowledgment. Legitimate orientation acknowledgment includes the affirmation of a singular's self-recognized orientation, permitting them to change their name and orientation marker on true archives, for example, ID cards, international IDs, and driver's licenses. This acknowledgment is urgent for certifying transsexual people's personalities and guaranteeing their full cooperation in different parts of society.

Argentina stands apart as a pioneer in lawful orientation acknowledgment. In 2012, the nation passed the Orientation Personality Regulation, spearheading a model for different countries. The law permits people to change their orientation marker on ID archives without the requirement for clinical mediations or legal endorsement. This dynamic regulation has been instrumental in advancing the freedoms and nobility of transsexual people in Argentina and has filled in as a motivation for comparable drives worldwide.

Be that as it may, legitimate orientation acknowledgment stays a challenged issue in many regions of the planet. In certain nations, the cycle is troublesome, requiring clinical mediations like chemical treatment or medical procedure, or endorsement from clinical experts. Such prerequisites can be obtrusive, pathologizing, and exclusionary, presenting boundaries to people who may not want or approach specific operations.

Transsexual people likewise face difficulties connected with medical care access. Orientation attesting medical services, which incorporates chemical treatment and orientation affirmation medical procedures, is fundamental for the majority transsexual people to adjust their actual appearance to their orientation personality. Admittance to equipped and confirming medical services is a basic part of transsexual privileges, as it straightforwardly influences the prosperity and emotional wellness of transsexual people.

Comprehensive and far reaching medical services approaches that cover orientation insisting therapies add to separating obstructions and guaranteeing that transsexual people can get to the consideration they need. Alternately, prejudicial medical care rehearses, for example, avoidances in protection inclusion for orientation avowing methodology, can worsen wellbeing differences and add to the minimization of transsexual people.

Legitimate assurances against separation in view of orientation character are central to guaranteeing the privileges and respect of transsexual people. Numerous nations and locales have presented enemy of segregation regulations that expressly incorporate orientation way of life as a safeguarded classification. These regulations expect to forestall segregation in different regions, including work, lodging, training, and public administrations.

In the US, the milestone choice in Bostock v. Clayton Area by the High Court in 2020 decided that Title VII of the Social liberties Act forbids segregation in view of sexual direction and orientation character. This choice denoted a huge triumph for LGBTQ+ privileges and confirmed that victimization transsexual people comprises sex segregation.

Regardless of lawful steps, transsexual people keep on confronting lopsided degrees of segregation and savagery, especially transsexual ladies of variety. Disdain violations focusing on transsexual people, combined with foundational issues like joblessness, vagrancy, and hindrances to medical care, feature the direness of tending to the diversity of these difficulties.

Diversity, an idea presented by Kimberlé Crenshaw, stresses the interconnected idea of social personalities and the intensifying impacts of various types of separation. For transsexual people, diversity perceives that their encounters are molded by their orientation way of life as well as by variables like race, identity, financial status, and inability.

Transsexual minorities, and especially transsexual ladies of variety, face elevated degrees of viciousness and segregation. The convergence of prejudice, transphobia, and sexism makes a perplexing trap of difficulties that require multifaceted promotion. Drives that focus on the encounters of transsexual people at the crossing points of various personalities are fundamental for making comprehensive and compelling arrangements and projects.

One remarkable region where multifacetedness is especially articulated is in the law enforcement framework. Transsexual people, particularly transsexual ladies of variety, are excessively addressed in the law enforcement framework and face elevated dangers of brutality, provocation, and unjustifiable treatment. Transsexual people in penitentiaries and detainment focuses frequently experience lacking medical services, seclusion, and savagery.

Endeavors to address the interconnection of transsexual freedoms include pushing for improvement in law enforcement, prejudicial arrangements, and elevating options in contrast to imprisonment. Associations that participate in multifaceted promotion work to enhance the voices of transsexual people with different characters and encounters, guaranteeing that arrangement arrangements are educated by the intricacy regarding their lived real factors.

Training assumes an essential part in progressing transsexual privileges and cultivating cultural acknowledgment. Comprehensive instructive educational plans that cover LGBTQ+ history and issues, including transsexual encounters, add to making a more educated and sympathetic culture. Preparing for teachers on making comprehensive and insisting spaces for transsexual understudies is fundamental for fighting segregation and cultivating a strong learning climate.

The battle for transsexual freedoms is unpredictably associated with the more extensive battle for LGBTQ+ fairness. Promotion endeavors frequently converge with those resolving issues like marriage correspondence, working environment segregation, and medical care access. The cooperative idea of these endeavors mirrors the common objective of making a general public that perceives and confirms the respect and freedoms, everything being equal, no matter what their orientation character or sexual direction.

Strict establishments play had a perplexing impact in molding mentalities toward transsexual people. While a few strict gatherings have embraced LGBTQ+ incorporation and certifying philosophy, others have been safe or straightforwardly threatening. Interfaith exchange and commitment look to connect these partitions, encouraging grasping, sympathy, and regard for the privileges and poise of transsexual people inside strict networks.

Web-based entertainment has arisen as an integral asset for transsexual promotion, giving a stage to people to share their accounts, interface with others, and bring issues to light about the difficulties they face. Hashtags, for example, #TransRightsAreHumanRights and #ProtectTransKids have built up some decent momentum, intensifying the voices of transsexual activists and partners and encouraging a feeling of local area and fortitude.

Worldwide associations and common freedoms bodies assume a basic part in progressing transsexual privileges on a worldwide scale. The Assembled Countries, through its Free and Rise to crusade, attempts to advance LGBTQ+ privileges, bring issues to light, and battle separation and savagery in view of sexual direction and orientation personality. Transsexual freedoms are additionally tended to inside the more extensive system of basic liberties and nondiscrimination.

Regardless of progress in specific locales, transsexual people in many areas of the planet keep on confronting lawful and cultural difficulties.

In certain nations, transsexual characters are condemned, and people might be dependent upon abuse, viciousness, or unfair regulations. Worldwide backing endeavors plan to address these basic freedoms infringement and advance lawful changes that certify the privileges of transsexual people universally.

4.4 Challenges and Progress in Achieving Equality

The quest for fairness, whether concerning orientation, race, sexual direction, or different aspects, is a continuous and multi-layered try set apart by the two difficulties and progress. This investigation digs into the intricacies of accomplishing balance, inspecting key deterrents and the steps made across different circles of society. From foundational treacheries to grassroots developments and regulative changes, the excursion toward fairness requires a nuanced comprehension of the obstacles confronted and the means taken to cultivate an additional equitable and comprehensive world.

At the core of the journey for fairness lies the acknowledgment of fundamental obstructions that propagate segregation and disparity. Underlying and institutional disparities manifest across different spaces, from instruction and work to medical services and law enforcement. Tending to these well established difficulties requires an extensive methodology that handles the fundamental designs sustaining disparity.

In the domain of orientation balance, fundamental orientation standards and generalizations keep on molding cultural assumptions and cutoff open doors for people in view of their orientation personality. Ladies, specifically, frequently face a bunch of difficulties, including the orientation pay hole, absence of portrayal in influential positions, and inconsistent admittance to training. Endeavors to challenge these fundamental issues include pushing for strategy changes, encouraging social moves, and destroying man centric standards that propagate orientation based separation.

Racial and ethnic incongruities further highlight the foundational idea of imbalance. Underestimated people group, particularly Dark, Native, and Ethnic minorities (BIPOC), fight with profoundly imbued primary bigotry that penetrates organizations, prompting variations in training, medical services, business, and law enforcement.

The battle for racial uniformity requests a supported obligation to destroying unfair strategies, tending to certain inclinations, and enhancing the voices of those excessively impacted by fundamental prejudice.

Sexual direction and orientation personality additionally cross with fundamental difficulties, as LGBTQ+ people explore oppressive regulations, social shame, and variations in medical care access. Accomplishing balance for the LGBTQ+ people group includes lawful changes, instruction drives, and encouraging comprehensive conditions that assert assorted characters. The battle against segregation in view of sexual direction or orientation personality is complicatedly connected to more extensive common freedoms support.

The handicap freedoms development correspondingly wrestles with fundamental hindrances, as people with inabilities stand up to availability difficulties, separation, and cultural misguided judgments. Accomplishing fairness for individuals with handicaps envelops pushing for general plan, comprehensive training, and testing ableism in the entirety of its structures. Perceiving the variety inside the incapacity local area and enhancing handicapped voices are critical parts of this continuous battle.

Instructive organizations act as the two milestones for equity and spaces where extraordinary change can flourish. Variations in admittance to quality training propagate patterns of imbalance, especially for underestimated networks. Tending to instructive imbalances includes fair financing, different and comprehensive educational programs, and establishing conditions that help the assorted requirements of understudies.

Governmental policy regarding minorities in society strategies, intended to address verifiable and foundational disparities, have been a wellspring of discussion. While defenders contend that governmental policy regarding minorities in society is a fundamental device for redressing past treacheries, rivals frequently raise worries about switch separation and legitimacy based confirmations. The talk encompassing governmental policy regarding minorities in society reflects more extensive discussions about the best techniques for accomplishing correspondence without sustaining new types of predisposition.

The work environment fills in as another field where uniformity fights unfurl. Orientation pay holes continue universally, with ladies procuring not exactly their male partners for identical work. Accomplishing pay value includes tending to wage differences as well as destroying fundamental hindrances that frustrate ladies' progression into positions of authority. Organizations embracing variety and consideration drives add to encouraging more impartial work environments.

Multifacetedness, an idea presented by Kimberlé Crenshaw, underscores the interconnected idea of social characters and the remarkable difficulties looked by people at the crossing points of various underestimated personalities. Recognizing multifacetedness is pivotal for creating comprehensive approaches and projects that address the complex and covering types of segregation experienced by people with crossing personalities.

The law enforcement framework reflects and sustains cultural imbalances, lopsidedly influencing underestimated networks. Racial profiling, over-policing, and brutal condemning add to the overrepresentation of BIPOC people in the law enforcement framework. Enhancement in law enforcement resolving foundational issues, for example, obligatory least sentences, cash bail, and the school-to-jail pipeline.

The unavoidable idea of imbalance stretches out to medical services, where minimized networks frequently face abberations in access and therapy. The Coronavirus pandemic featured existing wellbeing imbalances, with networks of variety encountering higher contamination and death rates. Accomplishing wellbeing value includes tending to the social determinants of wellbeing, guaranteeing fair admittance to medical care administrations, and fighting unfair practices inside the clinical field.

The Me Too development arose as a strong power in revealing insight into the pervasiveness of lewd behavior and attack, especially in the working environment. The development ignited a worldwide discussion about power elements, assent, and the unavoidable idea of orientation based savagery. While the Me Too development has prompted expanded mindfulness and a few institutional changes, challenges continue making enduring social moves that focus on security and responsibility.

Natural equity crosses with more extensive civil rights issues, featuring the unbalanced effect of ecological corruption on underestimated networks. Low-pay networks and networks of variety frequently endure the worst part of natural perils, from contamination to environmental change. Ecological equity support includes tending to these abberations and focusing the voices of those most impacted in conversations about reasonable and impartial arrangements.

The power elements intrinsic in cultural designs frequently manifest in political frameworks, where minimized networks might confront boundaries to cooperation and portrayal. Accomplishing political balance includes destroying elector concealment strategies, tending to manipulating, and cultivating comprehensive political spaces where different voices are heard and esteemed.

The job of innovation in sustaining or testing imbalance has become progressively critical. While innovation can possibly associate individuals, enhance minimized voices, and give admittance to data, it likewise reflects and can sustain existing inclinations.

Tending to computerized separates, advancing web access, and guaranteeing moral utilization of innovation are basic parts of a more fair mechanical scene.

The job of partners is instrumental in the battle for uniformity. Partners, people who backing and backer for underestimated networks without essentially sharing their characters, assume a vital part in enhancing voices, testing prejudicial practices, and cultivating comprehensive conditions. Allyship includes undivided attention, instruction, and a guarantee to destroying fundamental imbalances.

Lawful structures and strategy changes are fundamental devices chasing after balance. Social equality regulation, against segregation regulations, and basic liberties arrangements give the establishment to testing fundamental shameful acts. In any case, the viability of lawful measures relies upon their implementation, public mindfulness, and a pledge to tending to the underlying drivers of disparity.

Social developments have generally been impetuses for cultural change, testing standards, and pushing for uniformity. Developments, for example, the social liberties development, LGBTQ+ privileges development, and ladies' freedoms development have reshaped cultural mentalities and added to legitimate and strategy changes. Grassroots activism stays a strong power in considering organizations responsible and driving advancement.

Worldwide participation and fortitude are progressively urgent in tending to worldwide imbalances. Worldwide issues, for example, environmental change, pandemics, and relocation require cooperative endeavors that focus on the prosperity and freedoms, everything being equal, no matter what their identity or foundation. Global associations, deals, and collusions add to encouraging an additional interconnected and fair world.

In spite of the bunch difficulties, there have been eminent steps in the excursion toward balance. Marriage balance, headways in LGBTQ+ privileges, and the appointment of different political pioneers imply progress in testing unfair standards. The expanded perceivability of underestimated voices, worked with by virtual entertainment and grassroots developments, has added to moving cultural insights and needs.

Corporate social obligation has acquired conspicuousness as organizations perceive the significance of resolving social and ecological issues. Organizations participating in moral works on, supporting variety and consideration, and adding to local area prosperity add to a more even-handed and dependable business scene.

Instructive drives that advance sympathy, decisive reasoning, and social skill are necessary in encouraging a more comprehensive society. Schools and colleges assume a crucial part in molding people in the future and testing imbued predispositions.

Comprehensive instructive practices add to destroying generalizations, encouraging comprehension, and enabling understudies to become advocates for balance.

Human expression and media likewise assume a significant part in forming cultural stories and testing generalizations. Different and genuine portrayal in writing, film, and different types of media add to separating boundaries and cultivating sympathy. Social articulation turns into an integral asset for testing fundamental imbalances and advancing different viewpoints.

Chapter 5

Workers' Rights Movements

Laborers' Privileges Developments play had an essential impact in molding the cutting edge work scene, supporting for fair treatment, better working circumstances, and just remuneration. From the beginning of time, the battles of laborers have been set apart by aggregate endeavors to resolve foundational issues and lay out a structure that protects their freedoms. The foundations of these developments can be followed back to the Modern Unrest, a period set apart by huge social and monetary changes.

During the late eighteenth and mid nineteenth hundreds of years, the Modern Upset introduced another time of automated creation and urbanization. While these progressions achieved exceptional financial development, they likewise prompted unforgiving working circumstances, extended periods of time, and pitiful wages for the workforce. Because of these shameful acts, laborers started to arrange and advocate for their freedoms, establishing the groundwork for the specialists' privileges developments that would follow.

One of the earliest appearances of coordinated work activism was the Luddite development in mid nineteenth century Britain. The Luddites, a gathering of gifted material laborers, challenged the presentation of hardware that undermined their jobs. They accepted that the reception of computerized looms and different advancements would bring about employment misfortunes and lower compensation. The Luddite development, however eventually fruitless in stopping mechanical advancement, denoted an early case of laborers aggregately opposing ominous changes in their functioning circumstances.

As industrialization spread, so did the require laborers' freedoms. The work development picked up speed during the nineteenth 100 years, with the arrangement of worker's guilds and the push for administrative changes. In the US, the work development acquired conspicuousness in the late nineteenth hundred years, driven by the ascent of modern free enterprise. The Knights of Work, established in 1869, looked to join laborers across various exchanges and expertise levels. They supported for an eight-hour normal business day, better wages, and working environment a majority rules government.

Nonetheless, it was the American Organization of Work (AFL), laid out in 1886, that turned into a significant power in the work development. Driven by Samuel Gompers, the AFL zeroed in on putting together talented laborers into make based associations. The AFL's plan included aggregate bartering, worked on working circumstances, and the acknowledgment of laborers' freedoms. This undeniable a shift towards additional designated and key endeavors to address the particular necessities of various gatherings of laborers.

The battle for laborers' freedoms was not bound to the US. In the late nineteenth and mid twentieth hundreds of years, work developments arose across Europe, looking to resolve comparative issues connected with working circumstances, compensation, and the option to sort out. In the Unified Realm, the Worker's guild Congress (TUC) was laid out in 1868 to address the interests of laborers and direction aggregate haggling endeavors.

The turn of the twentieth century saw a flood in labor activism around the world. Occasions, for example, the Haymarket undertaking in 1886 and the Pullman Strike in 1894 featured the strains among work and capital. These occurrences likewise provoked a developing acknowledgment of the requirement for lawful insurances for laborers. In the US, milestone regulation, for example, the Fair Work Principles Demonstration of 1938 set guidelines for the lowest pay permitted by law, extra time pay qualification, recordkeeping, and kid work.

The worldwide effect of laborers' freedoms developments was additionally exemplified by the Russian Upheaval of 1917. The Trotskyites, drove by Vladimir Lenin, supported the reason for the working people and tried to lay out a communist society. While the Russian Transformation had expansive international results, its effect on laborers' privileges developments was critical, motivating comparative developments in different areas of the planet.

In the outcome of The Second Great War, laborers' freedoms developments built up forward movement in different nations. In Germany, the Weimar Republic presented moderate work regulations, perceiving the privileges of laborers to arrange and deal on the whole. Be that as it may, the financial difficulties of the interwar period additionally prompted expanded work agitation and the ascent of revolutionary philosophies.

The Economic crisis of the early 20s of the 1930s further powered the direness for laborers' privileges changes. In the US, President Franklin D. Roosevelt's New Arrangement programs incorporated the Public Work Relations Demonstration of 1935, otherwise called the Wagner Act. This regulation ensured the right of laborers to arrange and deal by and large. It additionally settled the Public Work Relations Board (NLRB) to administer work relations and address unreasonable work rehearses.

The Wagner Act denoted a huge achievement throughout the entire existence of laborers' freedoms, giving a lawful structure to aggregate bartering and shielding laborers from uncalled for work rehearses. It laid the foundation for the development of worker's organizations and the foundation of a more evenhanded harmony among work and the executives.

The mid-twentieth century saw the pinnacle of trade guild impact in the US. Associations like the Assembled Car Laborers (UAW) and the Unified Steelworkers (USW) arranged aggregate haggling arrangements that got higher wages, better working circumstances, and upgraded benefits for their individuals. The post-The Second Great War time saw an extension of the working class, halfway determined by the additions made by coordinated work.

In any case, the scene of laborers' privileges developments went through huge changes in the last 50% of the twentieth 100 years. The decay of conventional assembling ventures, the globalization of the economy, and changes in innovation presented difficulties to the customary model of modern unionism. The ascent of administration ventures and the gig economy introduced new intricacies for laborers looking to arrange and haggle aggregately.

The late twentieth century likewise saw a shift towards a more globalized way to deal with laborers' privileges. Worldwide associations like the Global Work Association (ILO) assumed a pivotal part in setting worldwide work guidelines and advancing civil rights. The ILO's Announcement on Central Standards and Privileges at Work, embraced in 1998, framed center work norms, including opportunity of affiliation, the right to aggregate haggling, and the end of constrained and youngster work.

The idea of corporate social obligation acquired unmistakable quality, encouraging organizations to consider the prosperity of laborers, networks, and the climate. Backing gatherings and non-administrative associations (NGOs) assumed a functioning part in considering enterprises responsible for their work rehearses. The rise of worldwide stock fastens likewise focused on issues, for example, sweatshop work and the requirement for global collaboration to address shifty working circumstances.

As the 21st century unfurled, new difficulties and open doors emerged for laborers' privileges developments. The advanced upheaval and the ascent of the gig economy introduced novel inquiries regarding the grouping and privileges of laborers in modern work game plans. Stages like Uber, Lyft, and TaskRabbit confronted investigation for their work works on, provoking discussions about the privileges of gig laborers and the requirement for refreshed work regulations.

The Coronavirus pandemic, which started in 2019, further highlighted the significance of laborers' freedoms. Fundamental specialists, including medical care experts, supermarket representatives, and conveyance drivers, confronted elevated takes a chance while offering pivotal types of assistance during lockdowns. The pandemic featured abberations in working environment wellbeing, professional stability, and admittance to medical care, provoking reestablished calls for upgraded laborers' freedoms and assurances.

In light of the difficulties presented by the developing idea of work, laborers' freedoms developments adjusted their procedures. Advanced putting together and virtual entertainment turned out to be incredible assets for activating specialists and bringing issues to light about work issues. Grassroots developments, for example, the Battle for $15 crusade supporting for a higher the lowest pay permitted by law, picked up speed and added to strategy changes in different purviews.

The idea of "specialist power" recovered conspicuousness, stressing the significance of engaging laborers to shape their functioning circumstances and supporter for their freedoms altogether. This approach tries to address power awkward nature among laborers and managers, perceiving the job of aggregate activity in accomplishing significant change.

The gig economy, described by present moment, independent, or on-request work, tested customary ideas of business connections. Laborers in the gig economy frequently missing the mark on securities stood to representatives, for example, the lowest pay permitted by law ensures, extra time pay, and admittance to benefits. Fights in court and authoritative endeavors looked to explain the business status of gig laborers and stretch out fundamental work assurances to this developing portion of the labor force.

The multifacetedness of laborers' privileges turned into a point of convergence in the 21st hundred years. Developments, for example, the Battle for $15 recognized the unbalanced effect of monetary disparity on minority and minimized networks. The accentuation on racial and orientation value inside the more extensive specialists' privileges plan featured the interconnectedness of civil rights issues.

The People of color Matter development, conceived out of a call for racial equity and a finish to police fierceness, likewise tended to financial variations and foundational imbalances in the work environment. The development caused to notice issues, for example, work environment segregation, wage holes, and the underrepresentation of ethnic minorities in administrative roles.

The Me Too development, at first centered around tending to inappropriate behavior and attack, extended its extension to incorporate working environment provocation and separation. The development highlighted the requirement for working environments to take on thorough strategies that advance a protected and comprehensive climate for all representatives.

5.1 The Labor Movement and Workers' Rights

The Work Development and Laborers' Privileges have been basic parts of the financial scene, with a set of experiences well established chasing fair treatment, worked on working circumstances, and impartial pay. These developments play had a crucial impact in molding the connection among managers and laborers, supporting for fundamental changes to guarantee the prosperity of the workforce. The development of the work development can be followed back to the Modern Unrest, a groundbreaking period that undeniable the shift from agrarian social orders to industrialized economies.

The Modern Transformation, which started in the late eighteenth 100 years, achieved critical mechanical progressions and financial development. In any case, it additionally brought about shifty working circumstances, with extended periods of time, low wages, and perilous work environments turning into the standard. Because of these difficulties, laborers started putting together and preparing for their freedoms, making way for the rise of the work development.

One of the earliest articulations of coordinated work opposition was the Luddite development in mid nineteenth century Britain. The Luddites, basically talented material specialists, challenged the presentation of hardware that compromised their occupations. They expected that robotization would prompt employment misfortunes and lower compensation, reflecting worries that resound with contemporary conversations about the effect of innovation on business. While the Luddite development didn't prevail with regards to ending mechanical advancement, it denoted a fundamental second in the aggregate opposition against troublesome working circumstances.

As industrialization spread across Europe and North America, laborers confronted unforgiving real factors in the processing plants and mines. The ascent of processing plant based creation frameworks supplanted customary high quality techniques, prompting a huge change in the idea of work. This progress energized the arrangement of worker's guilds and other work associations, laying the basis for additional organized endeavors to address the difficulties looked by laborers.

In the US, the mid-nineteenth century saw the rise of worker's organizations like the Knights of Work, established in 1869. The Knights of Work expected to join laborers across various exchanges and ability levels, supporting for an eight-hour business day, further developed wages, and working environment a majority rule government. While the Knights of Work experienced beginning achievement, it was the American Organization of Work (AFL), laid out in 1886 and drove by Samuel Gompers, that turned into a significant power in the work development. The AFL zeroed in on coordinating gifted laborers into make based associations, haggling for better circumstances and the acknowledgment of laborers' privileges.

The late nineteenth and mid twentieth hundreds of years saw a flood in labor activism universally. In the Unified Realm, the Worker's organization Congress (TUC) was established in 1868 to address the interests of laborers and direction aggregate dealing endeavors. Work developments in Europe tried to resolve issues connected with working circumstances, compensation, and the option to coordinate.

The battle for laborers' privileges picked up speed in the US, set apart by occasions, for example, the Haymarket issue in 1886 and the Pullman Strike in 1894. These occurrences highlighted the pressures among work and capital and featured the requirement for legitimate securities for laborers. In light of these difficulties, administrative changes started to come to fruition.

The mid twentieth century denoted a time of huge work change in the US. The Triangle Shirtwaist Production line fire in 1911, where 146 article of clothing laborers died because of perilous working circumstances, stirred popular assessment and prompted expanded requests for working environment security guidelines. The grievous occurrence highlighted the earnest requirement for complete work regulations to safeguard laborers.

The consequence of The Second Great War achieved further changes in the work scene. In Germany, the Weimar Republic presented moderate work regulations perceiving the privileges of laborers to sort out and deal aggregately. The Russian Insurgency of 1917, while principally a political disturbance, significantly affected specialists' privileges developments universally, rousing comparative developments and laying the basis for communist goals.

The Economic crisis of the early 20s of the 1930s exacerbated monetary difficulties, prompting expanded work distress. In the US, President Franklin D. Roosevelt's New Arrangement programs included milestone regulation, for example, the Public Work Relations Demonstration of 1935, otherwise called the Wagner Act. This regulation ensured laborers the option to arrange and deal on the whole, tending to uncalled for work rehearses and laying out the Public Work Relations Board (NLRB) to direct work relations.

The Wagner Act denoted a huge achievement, giving a legitimate system to aggregate haggling and shielding laborers from double-dealing. It added to the development of trade guilds and set up for a more impartial harmony among work and the executives. The mid-twentieth century saw the pinnacle of trade guild impact in the US, with associations arranging aggregate bartering arrangements that got higher wages, worked on working circumstances, and improved benefits for their individuals.

Be that as it may, the last 50% of the twentieth century achieved huge changes in the work scene. The decay of conventional assembling businesses, the globalization of the economy, and innovative progressions presented difficulties to the customary model of modern unionism. The ascent of administration enterprises and the gig economy introduced new intricacies for laborers looking to coordinate and haggle all in all.

The late twentieth century likewise saw a shift towards a more globalized way to deal with laborers' freedoms. Worldwide associations like the Worldwide Work Association (ILO) assumed a pivotal part in setting worldwide work norms and advancing civil rights. The ILO's Statement on Central Standards and Privileges at Work, embraced in 1998, framed center work principles, including opportunity of affiliation, the right to aggregate bartering, and the end of constrained and youngster work.

The idea of corporate social obligation acquired unmistakable quality, asking organizations to consider the prosperity of laborers, networks, and the climate. Promotion gatherings and non-legislative associations (NGOs) assumed a functioning part in considering enterprises responsible for their work rehearses. The development of worldwide inventory binds focused on issues, for example, sweatshop work, inciting global endeavors to address shifty working circumstances.

As the 21st century unfurled, new difficulties and valuable open doors arose for laborers' privileges developments. The computerized upheaval and the ascent of the gig economy introduced novel inquiries regarding the grouping and freedoms of laborers in modern work courses of action. Stages like Uber, Lyft, and TaskRabbit confronted investigation for their work works on, igniting banters about the privileges of gig laborers and the requirement for refreshed work regulations.

The Coronavirus pandemic, which started in 2019, further stressed the significance of laborers' freedoms. Fundamental laborers, including medical care experts, supermarket representatives, and conveyance drivers, confronted increased takes a chance while offering significant types of assistance during lockdowns. The pandemic featured differences in work environment wellbeing, professional stability, and admittance to medical services, provoking restored calls for upgraded laborers' freedoms and securities.

Because of the difficulties presented by the advancing idea of work, laborers' freedoms developments adjusted their methodologies. Computerized sorting out and web-based entertainment turned out to be integral assets for preparing laborers and bringing issues to light about work issues. Grassroots developments, for example, the Battle for $15 crusade supporting for a higher the lowest pay permitted by law, picked up speed and added to strategy changes in different locales.

The idea of "laborer power" recovered noticeable quality, underscoring the significance of engaging specialists to shape their functioning circumstances and supporter for their freedoms by and large. This approach tries to address power uneven characters among laborers and managers, perceiving the job of aggregate activity in accomplishing significant change.

The gig economy, described by present moment, independent, or on-request work, tested customary thoughts of business connections. Laborers in the gig economy frequently missing the mark on securities stood to representatives, for example, the lowest pay permitted by law ensures, additional time pay, and admittance to benefits. Fights in court and regulative endeavors looked to explain the business status of gig laborers and stretch out fundamental work assurances to this developing fragment of the labor force.

The multifacetedness of laborers' freedoms turned into a point of convergence in the 21st hundred years. Developments, for example, the Battle for $15 recognized the lopsided effect of financial disparity on minority and minimized networks. The accentuation on racial and orientation value inside the more extensive laborers' freedoms plan featured the interconnectedness of civil rights issues.

The People of color Matter development, conceived out of a call for racial equity and a finish to police ruthlessness, likewise tended to financial variations and foundational imbalances in the work environment. The development caused to notice issues, for example, working environment separation, wage holes, and the underrepresentation of minorities in administrative roles.

The Me Too development, at first centered around tending to lewd behavior and attack, extended its extension to incorporate working environment provocation and separation. The development highlighted the requirement for working environments to take on complete strategies that advance a protected and comprehensive climate for all representatives.

In the domain of innovation, the moral contemplations of computerized reasoning and mechanization provoked conversations about the possible effect on positions and laborers' freedoms. Worries about work uprooting and the requirement for retraining.

5.2 Contemporary Challenges in the Workplace

Contemporary difficulties in the working environment have developed close by mechanical progressions, evolving socioeconomics, and changes in cultural assumptions. As we explore the intricacies of the cutting edge workplace, issues like variety and incorporation, the effect of innovation on positions, emotional wellness and prosperity, and the gig economy have become noticeable worries.

Variety and consideration have ascended to the front of working environment discussions as of late. Associations are progressively perceiving the worth of different points of view and foundations in encouraging development and imagination. Notwithstanding, accomplishing genuine variety and consideration stays a test. Hindrances like oblivious predisposition, foundational disparities, unfair practices actually endure in numerous work environments.

Making a really comprehensive working environment requires recruiting a different labor force as well as encouraging a climate where all representatives feel esteemed and included. This includes resolving issues, for example, perceived hostilities, giving variety and consideration preparing, and carrying out arrangements that advance equivalent open doors for professional success. The push for variety and incorporation isn't simply an ethical objective yet additionally an essential business choice that can prompt superior hierarchical execution.

The effect of innovation on positions is another critical contemporary test. Robotization, man-made consciousness (simulated intelligence), and other innovative headways are changing ventures and occupation capabilities. While these advancements can possibly build effectiveness and efficiency, they likewise raise worries about work uprooting and the requirement for reskilling and upskilling.

Certain daily schedule and manual errands are progressively being computerized, influencing position in ventures, for example, assembling and client care. This mechanization pattern has prompted an interest for laborers with abilities in regions like information examination, programming, and critical thinking. Thus, there is a developing requirement for thorough labor force improvement projects to guarantee that representatives can adjust to the changing idea of work.

The gig economy, described by present moment, adaptable, and independent work courses of action, presents the two open doors and difficulties. Stages like Uber, Lyft, and TaskRabbit have re-imagined the idea of work, permitting people to partake in the economy on a more adaptable premise. Be that as it may, gig laborers frequently come up short on professional stability, advantages, and securities stood to customary workers.

The gig economy has ignited banters about the order of laborers and the requirement for refreshed work regulations. Finding some kind of harmony between the adaptability that gig work offers and the freedoms and securities that laborers merit has turned into a basic test. Policymakers are wrestling with inquiries concerning least wages, advantages, and aggregate haggling privileges for gig laborers, looking to make a system that guarantees fair treatment without smothering development.

Psychological wellness and prosperity have become progressively perceived as fundamental parts of a sound working environment. The quick moving, high-pressure nature of many positions, combined with the obscuring of limits among work and individual life because of innovation, has prompted developing worries about pressure, burnout, and psychological wellness issues.

Businesses are currently zeroing in on establishing conditions that focus on worker prosperity. This incorporates drives, for example, emotional wellness mindfulness programs, adaptable work game plans, and admittance to directing administrations. Perceiving the significance of emotional well-being adds to a more caring work environment as well as upgrades efficiency and representative maintenance.

Remote work, advanced by the Coronavirus pandemic, has turned into a huge part of the contemporary work scene. While remote work offers adaptability and the potential for further developed balance between fun and serious activities, it additionally brings difficulties like segregation, obscured limits among work and individual life, and the requirement for viable correspondence and coordinated effort instruments.

Associations are wrestling with how to make a cross breed work model that adjusts the advantages of remote work with the benefits of face to face joint effort. This includes resolving issues connected with innovation framework, group elements, and representative prosperity. The shift towards remote and half and half work game plans has long haul suggestions for how associations structure their activities and backing their labor force.

Network safety concerns have become progressively pervasive as the dependence on advanced innovations keeps on developing. The interconnectedness of frameworks and the tremendous measures of delicate information put away web-based convey associations helpless against digital intimidations. Information breaks, ransomware assaults, and other network safety occurrences can have serious outcomes, including monetary misfortunes and harm to notoriety.

Associations should put resources into strong online protection measures, including worker preparing, secure framework, and proactive danger recognition. As remote work turns out to be more common, getting the computerized climate turns out to be significantly more basic.

Adjusting the advantages of advanced change with the requirement for powerful network protection measures is quite difficult for associations across enterprises.

Work environment culture and representative commitment are perpetual difficulties that have taken on new aspects in the contemporary working environment. A positive working environment culture is significant for drawing in and holding ability, cultivating cooperation, and driving hierarchical achievement. Notwithstanding, making and keeping a solid culture requires deliberate exertion and a responsibility from initiative.

Representative commitment, which alludes to the close to home association workers have with their work and the association, is a vital figure efficiency and maintenance. The ascent of remote work and the advancing assumptions for the labor force require creative ways to deal with encouraging commitment. This incorporates ordinary correspondence, amazing open doors for ability advancement, and drives that line up with workers' qualities.

Natural maintainability has turned into a squeezing worry for associations as they perceive the effect of their procedure in the world. Environmental change, asset exhaustion, and ecological corruption have provoked a shift towards more supportable strategic policies. This includes diminishing carbon impressions, taking on eco-accommodating advances, and integrating maintainability into hierarchical qualities and systems.

Associations are progressively expected to exhibit natural obligation not exclusively to meet administrative necessities yet additionally to line up with the upsides of earth cognizant shoppers and representatives. Offsetting maintainability objectives with functional proficiency and monetary contemplations represents a test that requires key preparation and development.

The job of administration in exploring these contemporary difficulties is central. Pioneers should be versatile, ground breaking, and compassionate to actually resolve the assorted issues influencing the advanced working environment. This incorporates cultivating a culture of nonstop picking up, advancing variety and consideration, and showing a pledge to worker prosperity.

5.3 Globalization, Exploitation, and Fair Labor Practices

Globalization has been a groundbreaking power in the cutting edge world, associating economies, societies, and individuals across borders. While it has achieved financial development and expanded open doors, the peculiarity of globalization has additionally raised worries about abuse and fair work rehearses. The interconnectedness of the worldwide economy has made an intricate snare of connections between enterprises, laborers, and legislatures, requiring a nearer assessment of the moral elements of work rehearses on a worldwide scale.

One of the characterizing elements of globalization is the extension of worldwide partnerships (MNCs) that work across different nations. These enterprises frequently look for cost efficiencies by re-appropriating creation to nations with lower work costs. While this globalization of supply affixes has prompted financial improvement in numerous areas, it has likewise led to cases of double-dealing, as organizations explore different work principles and administrative conditions.

Shady work practices can take different structures, including low wages, long working hours, deficient security measures, and restricted freedoms for laborers to sort out. At times, MNCs might take advantage of contrasts in labor principles between nations, picking places where guidelines are careless, and work is more affordable. This rush to the base can prompt a competition to limit work costs without due respect for the prosperity of laborers.

The piece of clothing industry, for instance, has been a point of convergence of conversations on globalization and work double-dealing. Many design brands re-appropriate creation to nations with lower work costs, where laborers frequently face unfortunate working circumstances and get negligible wages. The Rana Square breakdown in Bangladesh in 2013, which brought about the passings of north of 1,100 article of clothing laborers, carried worldwide regard for the moral ramifications of reevaluating and the requirement for further developed work rehearses in the production network.

The idea of fair work rehearses has acquired conspicuousness as a re-action to the difficulties presented by globalization. Fair work rehearses incorporate a scope of standards, including the installment of living wages, sensible working hours, safe working circumstances, and the right of laborers to sort out and deal by and large. These standards mean to guarantee that specialists are treated with pride and regard, no matter what their geographic area or the business in which they work.

Worldwide associations, non-legislative associations (NGOs), and support bunches assume a pivotal part in advancing fair work rehearses universally. The Global Work Association (ILO), a particular organization of the Unified Countries, sets worldwide work principles and advances civil rights and good work for all. The ILO's center shows cover essential standards and privileges at work, including opportunity of affiliation, the right to aggregate dealing, the nullification of constrained work, and the disposal of kid work.

NGOs like the Fair Work Affiliation (FLA) and the Specialist Freedoms Consortium (WRC) work to screen and further develop work conditions in worldwide stockpile chains. These associations team up with organizations to guarantee that work principles are maintained and that specialists are dealt with morally. Through plant reviews,

reviews, and commitment with partners, these guard dog associations try to consider organizations responsible for the circumstances in their stock chains.

Corporate social obligation (CSR) has turned into a basic piece of the business scene, with many organizations perceiving the significance of moral and maintainable practices. CSR drives frequently incorporate responsibilities to fair work rehearses, ecological manageability, and local area commitment. Organizations that focus on CSR comprehend that capable strategic policies add to long haul achievement, improve brand notoriety, and relieve chances related with unscrupulous direct.

In any case, the viability of CSR drives differs, and pundits contend that a few organizations take part in "greenwashing" or "social washing" - utilizing shallow or misdirecting practices to make a positive picture without carrying out considerable changes. The strain between benefit intentions and moral contemplations stays a test, as organizations should adjust the requests of investors with their obligation to fair work rehearses.

Notwithstanding moral contemplations, fair work rehearses are additionally connected to more extensive issues of monetary disparity and civil rights. Globalization has added to critical monetary development in specific areas yet has additionally exacerbated pay imbalance inside and between nations. The double-dealing of modest work in non-industrial nations can propagate a pattern of destitution, restricting financial open doors for laborers and networks.

Endeavors to address worldwide work double-dealing require a multi-partner approach, including states, organizations, laborers, and common society. Legislatures assume a pivotal part in laying out and implementing work regulations that safeguard laborers' freedoms and guarantee fair wages and working circumstances. Nonetheless, challenges emerge when states come up short on limit or political will to actually authorize these guidelines.

Economic deals and worldwide collaboration systems likewise assume a part in forming fair work rehearses. Some contend that economic deals ought to incorporate arrangements that consider partaking nations responsible for maintaining work norms. Pundits, then again, express worries about the potential for such arrangements to be utilized as protectionist measures, possibly sabotaging the advantages of deregulation.

Specialist strengthening is a key part of tending to work double-dealing. The right of laborers to sort out, structure associations, and take part in aggregate dealing is fundamental for guaranteeing their voices are heard and their freedoms are safeguarded. In any case, in numerous nations, laborers face critical boundaries to sorting out because of hostile to association practices, terrorizing, and legitimate limitations. Fortifying specialists' freedoms to sort out is a basic move toward cultivating fair work rehearses.

Straightforwardness in supply chains is one more key component in tending to work double-dealing. Numerous buyers today are socially cognizant and need to go with moral buying choices.

Giving data about the beginning of items, the circumstances under which they were created, and the work practices of the organizations included empowers buyers to settle on informed decisions and comes down on enterprises to maintain fair work principles.

Mechanical headways, especially in the domain of blockchain and production network the executives frameworks, offer devices to improve straightforwardness. Blockchain, with its decentralized and alter safe nature, can be utilized to make straightforward and discernible stockpile chains. This innovation permits shoppers to confirm the realness of items and guarantees that organizations are considered responsible for their cases in regards to fair work rehearses.

Unofficial laws and industry-explicit drives can additionally advance straightforwardness. For instance, the California Straightforwardness in Supply Chains Act requires specific organizations to unveil their endeavors to kill subjection and illegal exploitation from their immediate stock chains. Comparable regulation in different wards adds to the worldwide development towards more noteworthy straightforwardness and responsibility in supply chains.

The job of buyers in driving change couldn't possibly be more significant. Moral commercialization, filled by an attention to fair work rehearses, can possibly impact partnerships to take on more dependable strategic policies. Virtual entertainment and online stages give a strong means to buyers to share data, prepare developments, and consider organizations responsible for their activities.

Regardless of progress in advancing fair work rehearses, critical difficulties endure. The intricacies of worldwide stock chains, contrasting administrative conditions, and financial tensions make snags to the inescapable execution of moral work rehearses. Accomplishing enduring change requires a responsibility from all partners - states, companies, laborers, and customers - to team up and maintain the standards of decency, pride, and regard for laborers across the globe.

All in all, globalization has reshaped the monetary scene, associating the world in remarkable ways. Nonetheless, the advantages of globalization accompany moral obligations, especially concerning fair work rehearses. Double-dealing as low wages, unfortunate working circumstances, and restricted laborers' privileges stays a test, especially as enterprises explore different administrative conditions and look for cost efficiencies. The advancement of fair work rehearses requires a multi-layered approach including worldwide associations, NGOs, backing gatherings, organizations, legislatures, and buyers. Moral commercialization, straightforward stockpile chains, and a guarantee to laborers' privileges are fundamental parts of a worldwide work to guarantee that the advantages of globalization are shared impartially, cultivating a reality where laborers are treated with nobility and regard, no matter what their geographic area.

5.4 Innovations in Workers' Advocacy

Developments in specialists' promotion play had an essential impact in reshaping the scene of work developments and tending to contemporary difficulties looked by laborers universally. As the idea of work develops and new types of business arise, imaginative ways to deal with laborers' support have become fundamental in upholding for fair treatment, worked on working circumstances, and the security of work freedoms.

One striking development in specialists' backing is the use of innovation to enhance the voices of laborers and work with aggregate activity. Computerized stages and web-based entertainment have become incredible assets for coordinating, preparing, and bringing issues to light about work issues. Grassroots developments, missions, and petitions can pick up speed quickly through web-based stages, empowering laborers to associate across geological limits and join in like manner causes.

The rise of laborer focused applications and computerized stages has given a way to laborers to get to data, report work environment mishandles, and interface with backing organizations. Applications like Coworker.org permit representatives to share their encounters, activate for aggregate activity, and backer for changes in working environment approaches. These stages engage laborers to take part effectively in molding their functioning circumstances and challenge out of line work rehearses.

Blockchain innovation is one more creative device with the possibility to reform laborers' support, especially with regards to production network straightforwardness. By utilizing blockchain, which gives a solid and straightforward record, associations can follow the creation and conveyance of products across complex inventory chains. This straightforwardness guarantees that work principles are maintained, and purchasers can settle on informed decisions in light of the moral acts of organizations.

Advancements in laborer driven innovation likewise incorporate the improvement of gig specialist stages that focus on fair treatment and enable laborers in the gig economy. Laborer claimed stages expect to give gig laborers better compensation, benefits, and a voice in direction. These stages are intended to address the difficulties looked by gig laborers, like absence of professional stability and admittance to benefits, by putting possession and control in the possession of the actual specialists.

Man-made reasoning (man-made intelligence) and AI advancements are progressively being utilized in laborers' support endeavors. These advances can examine immense measures of information to recognize examples of work freedoms infringement, wage burglary, and biased rehearses. Simulated intelligence devices can help with observing working environments, recognizing possible issues, and supporting legitimate endeavors to consider businesses responsible for work regulation infringement.

The gig economy, described by present moment, independent, or on-request work, has introduced extraordinary difficulties for customary types of laborers' promotion. Developments in promotion methodologies are vital for address the necessities of gig laborers who frequently miss the mark on conventional designs of associations. Compact advantages frameworks, which permit laborers to convey benefits with them across various gigs, are being investigated as an answer for give gig laborers admittance to medical services, retirement reserve funds, and other fundamental advantages.

One eminent illustration of advancement in gig laborers' backing is the improvement of convenient advantages stages. These stages expect to give gig laborers admittance to benefits generally connected with everyday work, for example, medical coverage, retirement designs, and took care of time. By decoupling benefits from explicit bosses, convenient advantages address the problematic idea of gig work and give a wellbeing net to laborers in the gig economy.

Legitimate advancements, for example, the foundation of sectoral haggling and compensation sheets, are being investigated as systems to address the difficulties presented by the gig economy. Sectoral haggling includes dealings among bosses and laborers across a whole industry, setting principles for wages and working circumstances that apply to all specialists inside that area. This approach recognizes the aggregate force of laborers in molding broad norms.

Laborer cooperatives address one more imaginative model in specialists' support. In a specialist helpful, the actual laborers own and control the business, settling on aggregate conclusions about its activity. This model enables laborers as well as adjusts monetary motivators to the prosperity of the labor force. Specialist cooperatives can be especially compelling in ventures with a serious level of occupation adaptability and independence, like consultants and gig laborers.

Organizations between customary trade guilds and new types of laborer associations have arisen as creative ways to deal with address the developing idea of work. Coordinated efforts among associations and specialist focuses, which are local area based associations supporting for the privileges of low-wage laborers, consider a more thorough and adaptable way to deal with laborers' promotion. These organizations influence the qualities of the two elements to address the novel difficulties looked by laborers in the advanced economy.

Advancements in laborer driven innovation likewise incorporate the improvement of gig specialist stages that focus on fair treatment and enable laborers in the gig economy. Laborer claimed stages expect to give gig laborers better compensation, benefits, and a voice in direction.

These stages are intended to address the difficulties looked by gig laborers, like absence of professional stability and admittance to benefits, by putting possession and control in the possession of the actual specialists.

Publicly supported information and specialist driven research have become useful assets in laborers' promotion endeavors. Stages that permit laborers to secretly share their encounters, report working environment infringement, and add to investigate drives empower a more far reaching comprehension of the difficulties looked by laborers. This information driven approach assists advocates with distinguishing designs, illuminate strategy suggestions, and fabricate a more grounded case for work freedoms implementation.

Vital suit has additionally advanced as an imaginative strategy in specialists' support. Public interest law offices and legitimate associations decisively use prosecution to challenge unreasonable work rehearses, advocate for strategy changes, and look for equity for laborers. High-profile cases and legal claims can cause to notice fundamental issues, brief regulative activity, and make points of reference that reinforce laborers' privileges.

The idea of "B Enterprises" or "Advantage Companies" addresses a development in corporate designs that puts social and natural objectives on fair terms with monetary targets. B Enterprises focus on gathering thorough social and ecological principles, including fair treatment of laborers, straightforwardness, and responsibility. This model urges organizations to take on mindful practices and contribute decidedly to society.

Worldwide partnerships and joint efforts among specialist associations have become progressively significant in tending to the globalized idea of work double-dealing. Organizations of laborer associations, NGOs, and support bunches team up across boundaries to share data, assets, and procedures. These worldwide partnerships enhance the aggregate voice of laborers and reinforce endeavors to consider global enterprises responsible for their work rehearses.

Developments in finance have likewise added to laborers' backing, especially in the domain of effect financial planning. Influence financial backers focus on speculations that produce positive social and natural results close by monetary returns. Putting resources into ventures that focus on fair work practices can add to the development of moral organizations and make a monetary environment that upholds laborers' freedoms.

The job of the scholarly world and examination establishments in laborers' promotion has extended through imaginative exploration strategies and associations with specialist associations. Participatory activity research, where laborers effectively add to the exploration cycle, guarantees that the viewpoints of those straightforwardly impacted by work issues are key to the examination. Scholastic coordinated efforts with specialist focuses and backing bunches assist with overcoming any issues among research and on-the-ground influence.

Social effect innovation stages, frequently created by charitable associations, influence innovation to address explicit work related difficulties. These stages might zero in on issues like compensation burglary, work environment separation, or admittance to legitimate assets. By giving specialists easy to use apparatuses and data, these stages enable people to grasp their privileges, report infringement, and look for help.

The diversity of laborers' backing has turned into a point of convergence, recognizing the interconnectedness of work issues with other civil rights concerns. Developments, for example, the Battle for $15, which advocates for a higher the lowest pay permitted by law, perceive the unbalanced effect of monetary disparity on minority and minimized networks. Incorporating racial and orientation value into the more extensive specialists' privileges plan mirrors a guarantee to tending to foundational disparities.

All in all, developments in laborers' backing are fundamental in adjusting to the advancing idea of work, the gig economy, and the difficulties presented by globalization. Innovation, lawful procedures, specialist driven stages, agreeable models, and worldwide joint efforts have reshaped the scene of laborers' backing, giving new instruments and ways to deal with address work privileges infringement. As the universe of work keeps on changing, the continuous turn of events and use of creative methodologies will be pivotal in propelling fair treatment, simply working circumstances, and the security of laborers' freedoms on a worldwide scale.

Chapter 6

Environmental Justice Movements

Ecological equity developments have acquired noticeable quality throughout the years as networks all over the planet wrestle with the results of natural debasement, contamination, and inconsistent circulation of natural advantages and weights. These developments look to address the interconnection of ecological issues and civil rights, underlining the requirement for fair and impartial treatment, everything being equal, no matter what their financial status, race, or geological area.

At the core of natural equity is the acknowledgment that specific networks, frequently minimized and disappointed, bear a lopsided weight of ecological mischief. This damage can appear in different structures, including openness to poisonous contaminations, absence of admittance to clean air and water, and weakness to the effects of environmental change. The development endeavors to redress these variations by supporting for strategies and practices that advance ecological value and guarantee that no local area is abandoned chasing an economical and solid future.

One of the essential standards of natural equity is the right to a solid climate. This right envelops the possibility that each person, no matter what their experience, has the option to reside locally where the air is perfect, the water is protected to drink, and the general climate upholds prosperity. Accomplishing ecological equity requires addressing authentic and fundamental imbalances that have prompted the centralization of natural dangers in specific networks, frequently populated by low-pay and minority occupants.

As a rule, ecological equity issues are established in a background marked by biased rehearses, for example, redlining, where networks of variety were deliberately denied admittance to assets and open doors. These verifiable treacheries have left an enduring effect, establishing conditions where weak populaces are bound to confront ecological dangers. Subsequently, the battle for natural equity is interlaced with more extensive battles for racial and financial equity.

To comprehend the advancement of ecological equity developments, it is fundamental to look at key crossroads in history that have molded the talk and pushed the progress ahead. The 1980s denoted a defining moment when networks of variety started preparing against the unbalanced siting of unsafe waste offices in their areas. The milestone instance of Warren Province, North Carolina, where occupants fought the development of a PCB landfill, exemplified the grassroots endeavors to challenge ecological prejudice.

The expression "ecological prejudice" acquired conspicuousness during this period to portray the fundamental act of finding natural dangers in networks with transcendently minority populaces. These people group frequently coming up short on political power and assets to actually oppose these sitings. The ecological equity development arose as a reaction to these treacheries, uniting activists, local area pioneers, and researchers to address the complicated transaction between the climate and social disparity.

As the development picked up speed, it extended its concentration to incorporate many natural issues, perceiving the interconnectedness of environmental and social frameworks. Environmental change turned into a focal worry, as its effects excessively influence weak networks.

From outrageous climate occasions to rising ocean levels, underestimated populaces frequently wind up on the forefronts of environment related calamities, confronting increased gambles and less assets to adapt to the repercussions.

The worldwide idea of natural difficulties has prompted the development of transnational ecological equity developments. These developments perceive that natural issues rise above public boundaries and require cooperative endeavors to actually address. Grassroots associations, backing gatherings, and native networks from various regions of the planet have met up to share information, assets, and techniques for advancing natural equity on a worldwide scale.

Native people group assume a significant part in the ecological equity development, as they frequently have a profound association with the land and are lopsidedly impacted by natural corruption. The development recognizes the significance of native information and looks to enhance native voices in dynamic cycles connected with natural approaches. Native drove developments, for example, the Standing Stone fights against the Dakota Access Pipeline, stand out and featured the continuous battles for land freedoms and natural equity.

As well as tending to the inconsistent dissemination of ecological weights, the natural equity development advocates for the fair circulation of natural advantages. This incorporates admittance to green spaces, clean energy, and economical advancement open doors. By advancing strategies that focus on the prosperity, everything being equal, the development plans to make an additional comprehensive and simply natural future.

Government strategies and guidelines assume a pivotal part in forming ecological equity results. The development requires the authorization of existing ecological regulations and the making of new approaches that unequivocally address the necessities of minimized networks. Ecological equity advocates work to consider enterprises responsible for their natural effect and request that administrative organizations think about the combined impacts of contamination on weak populaces.

The battle for natural equity is additionally firmly connected to the more extensive battle for vote based independent direction and local area strengthening. Numerous natural equity fights include networks affirming their entitlement to take part in the dynamic cycles that influence their lives. This incorporates moving hierarchical ways to deal with ecological approach and supporting for local area driven arrangements that mirror the special requirements and viewpoints of those straightforwardly affected.

Instructive drives are an essential part of the natural equity development, planning to bring issues to light about the convergence of ecological issues and civil rights. These endeavors try to engage people to comprehend and address the natural difficulties confronting their networks effectively. By cultivating ecological education, the development urges individuals to become advocates for change and partake in molding arrangements that advance equity and maintainability.

Natural equity developments have effectively affected arrangement changes at different degrees of government. From neighborhood statutes to peaceful accords, the development's support has prompted more prominent acknowledgment of the significance of integrating value into ecological independent direction. In any case, challenges endure, and the development keeps on pushing for additional thorough and enforceable arrangements that address the main drivers of natural unfairness.

The ecological equity development faces resistance from strong interests that advantage from the norm. Businesses liable for ecological mischief frequently oppose guidelines that would expect them to take on cleaner works on, outlining such measures as dangers to financial development. Conquering these difficulties requires building expansive alliances that unite assorted partners, including naturalists, worker's organizations, and local gatherings.

Natural equity is intrinsically connected to monetary equity, as underestimated networks frequently endure the worst part of both ecological and financial imbalances. The development advocates for the making of green positions and practical financial open doors that focus on friendly and natural prosperity. By advancing monetary options that don't depend on the double-dealing of regular assets and weak networks, the development looks to fabricate a stronger and fair economy.

Natural equity developments likewise feature the significance of tending to the main drivers of ecological corruption, including overconsumption and impractical asset extraction. The quest for interminable monetary development, combined with an expendable culture, adds to ecological mischief and worsens social disparities. The development requires a shift towards additional supportable and regenerative practices that regard the World's biological cutoff points.

Local area based arrangements are at the very front of the ecological equity development, perceiving that neighborhood information and commitment are fundamental for making enduring change. From people group nurseries to sustainable power projects, grassroots drives exhibit the potential for individuals to assume command over their natural fate. These tasks add to supportability as well as cultivate a feeling of strengthening and aggregate organization inside networks.

The ecological equity development crosses with other civil rights developments, making a strong organization of promoters pursuing an additional fair and practical world. Cooperation with developments tending to racial equity, orientation uniformity, and native privileges enhances the effect of aggregate endeavors. The acknowledgment that social and ecological equity are interconnected builds up the possibility that a genuinely impartial society should address fundamental treacheries on different fronts.

The media assumes a urgent part in forming public discernment and impacting strategy conversations connected with ecological equity. The development endeavors to intensify the voices of impacted networks and challenge one-sided accounts that propagate ecological bigotry. By advancing precise and comprehensive portrayals of ecological issues, the development intends to assemble public help for arrangements that focus on equity and supportability.

Ecological equity developments likewise influence the force of narrating to acculturate the effects of natural debasement. Individual stories and local area stories give a useful asset to interfacing with crowds on a close to home level, encouraging sympathy, and motivating activity. Through narratives, writing, and workmanship, the development looks to connect with a more extensive crowd and prepare public help for groundbreaking change.

Lately, youth-drove developments, like Fridays for Future and the Dawn Development, have carried reestablished energy to the ecological equity development. Youthful activists, propelled by figures like Greta Thunberg, have prepared huge number of individuals overall to request earnest activity on environmental change and natural equity. The adolescent drove development underscores the intergenerational idea of ecological equity, featuring the ethical basic to safeguard the planet for people in the future.

Innovation and development likewise assume a part in progressing natural equity objectives. From satellite imaging to local area driven natural observing, innovative apparatuses engage networks to accumulate information and proof of ecological mischief. This data can be instrumental in fights in court and backing endeavors, considering polluters responsible and supporting the call for more grounded ecological guidelines.

Notwithstanding the headway made by the ecological equity development, huge difficulties remain. The continuous battle for equity in networks like Rock, Michigan, where occupants keep on wrestling with the effects of lead-sullied water, highlights the requirement for supported promotion and foundational change. The development faces the continuous danger of co-optation, where good natured drives are co-picked by strong interests, prompting watered-down arrangements that neglect to address underlying drivers.

Ecological equity developments additionally battle with the worldwide idea of natural difficulties. Resolving issues like deforestation, biodiversity misfortune, and environmental change requires worldwide collaboration and composed endeavors. The development explores the pressure between nearby needs and the requirement for worldwide arrangements, stressing the significance of fortitude and shared liability chasing ecological equity.

As the ecological equity development keeps on advancing, it should wrestle with arising issues, like the convergence of innovation and natural equity. The ascent of savvy urban areas, man-made brainpower, and the Web of Things presents new difficulties and potential open doors. Guaranteeing that innovative progressions add to, instead of fuel, natural equity concerns requires proactive commitment and support.

The legitimate system encompassing ecological equity is a basic landmark for the development. Ecological equity advocates work to reinforce and authorize regulations that shield weak networks from natural mischief.

This incorporates testing unfair drafting works on, upholding for the right to a sound climate in lawful settings, and considering legislatures and companies responsible for ecological treacheries.

The job of the scholarly community is additionally critical in propelling the objectives of the natural equity development. Examination and grant add to a more profound comprehension of the mind boggling elements between ecological issues and civil rights. Scholastics took part in natural equity work give significant bits of knowledge that illuminate strategy conversations and shape the story around the requirement for extraordinary change.

Ecological equity developments perceive the significance of cultivating a feeling of interconnectedness with nature. Native perspectives and conventional natural information underline the reliance of every single living being and the requirement for an agreeable relationship with the Earth. Integrating these viewpoints into the more extensive natural equity development enhances how its might interpret manageability and versatility.

The idea of "simply changes" has built up some decent momentum inside the natural equity development, underscoring the requirement for an impartial and comprehensive progress to a supportable future. Simply advances perceive that the shift away from non-renewable energy sources and other ecologically unsafe practices should focus on the prosperity of laborers and networks as of now reliant upon these enterprises. This approach looks to try not to rehash the authentic shameful acts related with financial advances.

Ecological equity developments likewise draw in with the idea of natural restitutions, perceiving that specific networks have borne the brunt of ecological damage for ages. Calls for repayments incorporate requests for pay, remediation, and the option to partake in dynamic cycles that influence the eventual fate of impacted networks. This part of the development challenges existing power designs and requires a rearrangement of natural advantages and weights.

The diversity of natural equity is obvious in the acknowledgment that various networks face exceptional difficulties in view of their particular settings. Metropolitan people group might wrestle with issues of air and water contamination, while country networks might confront the effects of modern horticulture and asset extraction. The development underlines the requirement for custom-made arrangements that address the particular natural equity worries of every local area.

6.1 Linking Environmental Issues to Social Injustice

Connecting ecological issues to social bad form enlightens the many-sided associations between the prosperity of the planet and the impartial treatment of assorted human networks. This diversity highlights the truth that ecological difficulties are not appropriated consistently across society; all things being equal, they frequently worsen existing social imbalances. From admittance to clean air and water to the effects of environmental change, the connection between ecological issues and social shamefulness appears in complex ways, molding the stories of various networks around the world.

Admittance to natural assets, for example, clean air and water, fills in as a strong illustration of how ecological issues converge with civil rights. All things considered, underestimated networks, frequently made out of low-pay people and minorities, bear a lopsided weight of contamination and ecological debasement. The siting of modern offices and dangerous waste destinations in these networks sustains a pattern of ecological shamefulness, prompting unfriendly wellbeing impacts and lessened personal satisfaction.

Networks confronting natural treachery habitually experience more elevated levels of respiratory ailments, cardiovascular infections, and other wellbeing differences. The absence of admittance to medical services assets further mixtures these difficulties, making a situation where weak populaces face a twofold weight of ecological and wellbeing disparities. The idea of natural prejudice suitably portrays this peculiarity, stressing the foundational and biased situation of ecological perils in networks with a higher level of minorities.

Discriminatory openness to contamination isn't exclusively a consequence of luck; it is in many cases established in verifiable and fundamental variables. Practices, for example, redlining, which deliberately denied monetary administrations to neighborhoods in view of racial organization, added to the centralization of weak networks in regions with natural dangers. These authentic treacheries keep on resonating through ages, molding the natural real factors looked by changed segment gatherings.

Environmental change, a worldwide ecological test, further highlights the diversity of natural issues and civil rights. While the effects of environmental change are felt all around, weak networks endure the worst part of its belongings all the more harshly. Low-pay networks, frequently situated in flood-inclined regions or areas defenseless to outrageous climate occasions, wind up on the bleeding edge of environment related calamities, confronting elevated chances and less assets to adapt to the consequence.

The worldwide idea of environmental change requires an aggregate and comprehensive reaction that thinks about the differential weaknesses of different gatherings. Native people group, for example, frequently experience the effects of environmental change all the more intensely because of their nearby association with the land. Rising ocean levels, changing atmospheric conditions, and interruptions to biological systems compromise their conventional lifestyles as well as their social legacy.

Connecting ecological issues to social bad form requires perceiving the job of force elements in molding who bears the weights of natural mischief and who benefits from ecological assets. The expression "natural honor" epitomizes the possibility that specific gatherings partake in the advantages of a solid climate while others get through the outcomes of ecological debasement. This honor is frequently entwined with financial status, race, and geological area, making distinct differences in natural prosperity.

Ecological honor appears in different ways, including admittance to green spaces, clean energy, and feasible advancement open doors. Princely people group might appreciate very much kept up with parks, proficient public transportation, and cleaner air, while underestimated networks face the difficulties of natural debasement and deficient foundation. This divergence in ecological honor reflects and propagates more extensive social disparities.

Administration and dynamic cycles assume a vital part in figuring out who has the ability to shape natural strategies and practices. Ecological dynamic that needs inclusivity and straightforwardness can additionally worsen social shameful acts. Networks that are most impacted by natural issues should have a significant seat at the table, permitting them to contribute their points of view and mastery to the dynamic interaction.

The connection between ecological issues and social shamefulness is additionally apparent in the uprooting and loss of land experienced by numerous networks. Lopsidedly impacted by modern activities, extractive ventures, and enormous scope improvement, underestimated networks frequently end up constrained off their familial terrains. This relocation disturbs networks' social texture as well as adds to the deficiency of social legacy and personality.

Native people group, specifically, face the infringement of their property freedoms, frequently encountering natural treacheries because of asset extraction on their domains. The battle for land privileges is naturally attached to the more extensive battle for ecological equity, as these networks look for not exclusively to safeguard their properties yet in addition to save their extraordinary associations with the climate and guarantee intergenerational maintainability.

Connecting natural issues to social treachery includes perceiving the job of ecological debasement in propagating patterns of neediness. Weak people group, needing admittance to assets and chances, frequently end up in conditions with restricted financial possibilities. The corruption of regular assets further reduces these networks' capacity to support themselves, making an input circle of neediness and ecological damage.

Financial exercises that add to ecological corruption, like deforestation, overfishing, and contamination, excessively influence underestimated networks that depend on normal assets for their occupations. The double-dealing of these assets without respect for ecological maintainability further digs in friendly imbalances, making a situation where those with more prominent monetary power keep on benefitting to the detriment of weak populaces.

In connecting ecological issues to social foul play, it is fundamental to recognize the job of the worldwide monetary framework in propagating natural mischief. The quest for perpetual financial development frequently depends on impractical asset extraction, adding to natural debasement and social disparity.

The prioritization of benefit over natural and social prosperity makes a framework where the expenses of ecological damage are externalized onto minimized networks.

The idea of ecological imperialism develops these elements, featuring how strong countries and enterprises exploit the regular assets of less strong areas, frequently to the impairment of neighborhood environments and networks. The natural results of such abuse, from deforestation to water contamination, lopsidedly influence the most helpless, showing the interconnectedness of worldwide financial frameworks and ecological equity.

Ecological equity developments underscore the requirement for a change in outlook towards additional supportable and fair monetary frameworks. This shift includes testing the predominant account that financial advancement should come to the detriment of the climate and underestimated networks. All things being equal, the development calls for financial models that focus on friendly and ecological prosperity, encouraging versatility and supportability.

Innovation and development assume a double part in the crossing point of ecological issues and civil rights. While mechanical headways can possibly address natural difficulties, they likewise raise worries about who benefits from these developments and who bears the dangers. The sending of specific advancements, like waste incinerators or reconnaissance frameworks, frequently happens in minimized networks, adding to ecological shamefulness.

Ecological equity developments draw in with the capability of innovation to engage networks in checking and resolving natural issues. From people group driven natural checking activities to the utilization of satellite symbolism, innovation can give significant apparatuses to social occasion information, considering polluters responsible, and supporting for strategy changes. Nonetheless, guaranteeing that these advances serve the interests of minimized networks requires cautious thought of force elements and inclusivity.

The connection between natural issues and social treachery is likewise clear in the inconsistent dissemination of the advantages of sustainable power. While the progress to clean energy is fundamental for moderating environmental change, the organization of sustainable power foundation can prompt natural improvement. Well-off networks frequently receive the rewards of sustainable power projects, for example, work creation and admittance to clean energy, while weak networks might confront the adverse consequences, like disturbances to neighborhood environments and scenes.

Natural equity developments advocate for a simply change to environmentally friendly power that focuses on the consideration of impacted networks in dynamic cycles and guarantees fair conveyance of advantages. This includes testing the hierarchical methodologies that have portrayed some sustainable power activities and underlining local area driven arrangements that line up with the interesting necessities and needs of every local area.

6.2 Communities on the Frontlines of Environmental Challenges

Networks on the bleeding edges of ecological difficulties are at the very front of the effects of natural debasement, environmental change, and modern contamination. These people group, frequently underestimated and powerless, bear an unbalanced weight of the pessimistic outcomes related with ecological issues. From the infringement of modern offices to the staggering impacts of environment related debacles, these bleeding edge networks face exceptional and frequently serious difficulties that request consideration, compassion, and coordinated endeavors for alleviation and variation.

Modern exercises and the siting of dangerous offices have generally lopsidedly impacted minimized networks. This training, frequently alluded to as ecological bigotry, features the purposeful arrangement of naturally unsafe exercises in regions populated by minorities and low-pay occupants. The outcome is that these networks become presented to more significant levels of air and water contamination, harmful material, and other ecological risks, prompting antagonistic wellbeing impacts.

One of the main attributes of networks on the forefronts is their absence of political and financial power. These people group frequently face boundaries to powerful cooperation in dynamic cycles that decide the position of modern offices and the authorization of ecological guidelines. The shortfall of a solid voice in these issues leaves these networks helpless against ecological treacheries, supporting more extensive examples of social imbalance.

The geological dissemination of natural dangers isn't arbitrary but instead reflects authentic and fundamental practices. The idea of redlining, a biased practice in lodging and loaning that efficiently prevented assets to networks from getting variety, has added to the convergence of weak networks in regions with higher natural dangers. This authentic heritage highlights the need to address the underlying drivers of natural treachery implanted in prejudicial acts of the past.

Environmental change intensifies the difficulties looked by networks on the bleeding edges. Outrageous climate occasions, rising ocean levels, and changes in precipitation designs excessively influence weak networks that frequently miss the mark on assets to adjust. Seaside people group, for example, face the double danger of modern contamination and the expanded recurrence and power of typhoons and tempest floods. The intensifying impacts of ecological debasement and environmental change cause what is happening for these bleeding edge networks.

Native people group, specifically, are frequently on the bleeding edges of both ecological corruption and environmental change. Their profound association with the land makes them especially powerless against changes in biological systems and the disturbance of conventional lifestyles.

The double-dealing of regular assets, like deforestation and asset extraction, further undermines the livelihoods and social legacy of native networks. Perceiving the freedoms of native people groups and integrating their customary information into ecological direction is essential for tending to these interconnected difficulties.

Networks on the forefronts of natural difficulties additionally face issues of ecological uprooting and loss of land. The infringement of modern exercises frequently prompts the removal of occupants, especially those in low-pay and underestimated networks. This removal disturbs social designs as well as adds to the deficiency of social character and local area attachment. Guaranteeing the option to remain in one's genealogical land and safeguarding against constrained dislodging is necessary to the more extensive battle for natural equity.

The idea of natural equity underlines the fair treatment, everything being equal, paying little heed to race, identity, or financial status, in ecological navigation. Notwithstanding, people group on the forefronts frequently experience ecological shameful acts, with their voices minimized in conversations about the effects of strategies and ventures on their lives. This absence of incorporation propagates a pattern of ecological disparity, where those most impacted have minimal impact over choices that shape their current circumstance.

Natural equity developments effectively work to enhance the voices of networks on the cutting edges, perceiving the significance of incorporating those straightforwardly affected in dynamic cycles. Grassroots associations, local area pioneers, and activists team up to advocate for strategies that address the particular requirements of cutting edge networks. This includes provoking hierarchical ways to deal with natural navigation and supporting local area driven arrangements that mirror the interesting viewpoints and needs of those on the bleeding edges.

Admittance to spotless and safe water is an essential basic liberty, yet numerous networks on the forefronts face difficulties connected with water defilement and shortage. Modern contamination, farming spillover, and deficient framework add to water quality issues that excessively influence underestimated networks. Stone, Michigan, became significant of this emergency when inhabitants, generally African American, were presented to lead-sullied water because of government carelessness and cost-cutting measures.

Water equity is an essential part of the more extensive ecological equity system. Guaranteeing impartial admittance to clean water requires tending to the main drivers of defilement and carrying out strategies that focus on the prosperity of cutting edge networks. From addressing maturing framework to considering polluters responsible, the battle for water equity crosses with more extensive battles for ecological and civil rights.

Air quality is one more basic worry for networks on the cutting edges. Closeness to modern offices, interstates, and other contamination sources opens inhabitants to more elevated levels of air poisons, prompting respiratory sicknesses and other wellbeing variations. The weight of air contamination falls excessively on low-pay networks and networks of variety, showing the multifacetedness of natural and social disparities.

Cutting edge networks frequently experience an absence of green spaces and ecological conveniences that add to generally speaking prosperity. Princely areas might appreciate very much kept up with parks and sporting facilities, while underestimated networks might need admittance to such assets. The shortfall of green spaces influences actual wellbeing as well as reduces the general personal satisfaction for occupants here.

Ecological equity developments advocate for strategies that focus on the creation and support of green spaces in cutting edge networks. These drives expect to address verifiable variations in admittance to nature and advance ecological conveniences that improve the wellbeing and flexibility of minimized networks. Local area gardens, metropolitan green spaces, and reforestation endeavors become essential parts of the more extensive methodology for ecological equity.

The effect of ecological difficulties on general wellbeing is a critical worry for networks on the bleeding edges. Openness to poisons, tainted water, and corrupted conditions add to higher paces of respiratory sicknesses, cardiovascular illnesses, and other wellbeing inconsistencies. The absence of admittance to medical care assets further fuels these difficulties, making a situation where weak populaces face a twofold weight of ecological and wellbeing treacheries.

The Coronavirus pandemic has highlighted the interconnectedness of general wellbeing and ecological equity. Weak people group, previously confronting wellbeing variations, have borne an unbalanced weight of the pandemic's effects. The pandemic has featured the direness of tending to foundational disparities and guaranteeing that cutting edge networks have evenhanded admittance to medical services assets, including testing, therapy, and immunization.

Ecological equity developments underline the significance of tending to the main drivers of natural and wellbeing incongruities. This includes testing the practices and strategies that add to natural mischief and pushing for fundamental changes that focus on the prosperity of bleeding edge networks. From stricter guidelines on modern contamination to local area drove drives for ecological checking, the battle for natural equity meets with more extensive endeavors to advance general wellbeing value.

Monetary variations further compound the difficulties looked by networks on the bleeding edges of ecological issues. These people group frequently need monetary chances, confronting higher paces of joblessness and underemployment.

The double-dealing of normal assets without respect for ecological maintainability adds to the pattern of destitution and natural mischief, making a situation where those with more prominent monetary power keep on benefitting to the detriment of weak populaces.

Ecological equity developments advocate for the production of green positions and maintainable monetary open doors that focus on friendly and natural prosperity. The progress to environmentally friendly power, for instance, presents an open door to address environmental change as well as set out business open doors in cutting edge networks. By advancing financial choices that don't depend on the double-dealing of regular assets and weak networks, the development looks to fabricate a stronger and fair economy.

The natural equity development likewise draws in with the idea of "simply changes." This approach stresses the requirement for a fair and comprehensive progress to an economical future. Simply changes perceive that the shift away from petroleum products and other earth unsafe practices should focus.

6.3 Indigenous Perspectives on Environmental Justice

Native points of view on ecological equity offer significant experiences into the perplexing connections between human networks and the regular world. Attached in profound associations with the land,

Native information frameworks underline the reliance of every living being and advocate for manageable and agreeable collaborations with the climate. Be that as it may, Native people group around the world face tireless difficulties, including ecological debasement, infringement of land freedoms, and the effects of environmental change. Understanding and integrating Native points of view is significant for progressing natural equity and encouraging a more practical connection among mankind and the planet.

At the center of Native viewpoints on ecological equity is the acknowledgment of the Earth as a living substance with intrinsic worth. Native perspectives view the regular world not just as an asset to be taken advantage of however as a wellspring of life and insight. The land, water, and air are basic pieces of a complicated trap of connections that support every living being. This comprehensive comprehension illuminates Native ways to deal with ecological stewardship, underlining the significance of equilibrium and correspondence.

Native people group frequently express a profound feeling of obligation for the prosperity of the land and people in the future. This intergenerational point of view perceives the need to settle on choices that think about the drawn out influences on the climate. Practices like customary biological information, went down through ages, give significant bits of knowledge into economical asset the executives, biodiversity preservation, and variation to changing natural circumstances.

The idea of "seventh era thinking" is a core value in numerous Native societies, stressing the possibility that choices made today ought to consider their impacts on the prosperity of the seventh era into what's to come. This forward-looking point of view diverges from present moment, shifty practices that can prompt natural corruption and treachery. Integrating seventh era thinking into more extensive ecological strategies lines up with the objectives of manageability and flexibility.

Land is integral to Native personality, culture, and otherworldliness. Numerous Native people group keep up with consecrated destinations and participate in otherworldly practices intently attached to explicit scenes. The dispossession of Native grounds, whether through verifiable treacheries or contemporary practices, addresses an immediate attack on the social and profound underpinnings of these networks. Natural equity, according to a Native point of view, includes not just tending to the actual effects of ecological debasement yet additionally perceiving and regarding the profound meaning of the land.

Native land freedoms are principal to the battle for ecological equity. By and large, colonization and expansionist arrangements have prompted the constrained expulsion of Native people groups from their hereditary grounds. This dispossession has frequently been joined by ecological corruption as customary practices are disturbed, prompting the abuse of normal assets without respect for maintainability. Perceiving and regarding Native land privileges is a urgent move toward redressing verifiable treacheries and advancing ecological equity.

The double-dealing of regular assets on Native grounds, frequently without the free, earlier, and educated assent regarding Native people group, stays a tenacious issue. Extractive enterprises, like mining, logging, and oil boring, can have extreme natural and social effects, upsetting biological systems, debasing water sources, and sabotaging conventional vocations. Native people group wind up on the forefronts of these ecological difficulties, confronting the results of asset extraction without receiving the rewards.

The battle for ecological equity according to a Native viewpoint includes testing the acts of enterprises and states that exploit regular assets on Native grounds. Native drove developments, for example, the obstruction against the Dakota Access Pipeline at Standing Stone, represent the continuous battle to safeguard holy locales, guard land freedoms, and guarantee that choices about asset extraction regard Native sway. These developments additionally require the consideration of Native viewpoints in ecological dynamic cycles.

Natural equity crosses with more extensive battles for Native privileges, including language protection, social rejuvenation, and self-assurance. The protection of Native dialects is fundamental to keeping up with customary biological information and giving it to people in the future. Language epitomizes the association among individuals and the climate, and the deficiency of dialects adds to the disintegration of Native information frameworks.

Social renewal endeavors, including conventional services, narrating, and workmanship, assume a urgent part in building up the association between Native people group and the climate. These social practices not just add to the flexibility of Native character yet additionally act as systems for communicating biological information, encouraging ecological stewardship, and opposing the eradication of Native societies.

Self-assurance, a primary standard in the battle for Native freedoms, incorporates the option to control and oversee normal assets on conventional terrains. Enabling Native people group to arrive at conclusions about their current circumstance lines up with the standards of ecological equity, guaranteeing that those most impacted by natural issues have organization in molding arrangements. Native drove protection drives and feasible asset the board projects represent the crossing point of self-assurance and natural equity.

Environmental change presents interesting difficulties for Native people group, as they frequently occupy naturally weak regions. The effects of environmental change, including climbing temperatures, changes in precipitation designs, and the expanded recurrence and power of outrageous climate occasions, straightforwardly influence conventional livelihoods and biological systems. Waterfront Native people group face the dangers of rising ocean levels and tempest floods, while Cold people group wrestle with the quick loss of ocean ice and disturbances to conventional hunting rehearses.

Native viewpoints on environmental change underline the interconnectedness of ecological, social, and social aspects. Environmental change isn't exclusively a natural issue however a significant test to the texture of Native people group. The deficiency of ice, changes in transitory examples of creatures, and modifications to establish cycles upset customary practices and compromise the endurance of Native lifestyles.

Relieving and adjusting to environmental have a significant impact on according to a Native viewpoint includes a comprehensive methodology that perceives the interdependencies among biological systems and networks. Native information frameworks, established in perceptions of the regular world over ages, offer important bits of knowledge into versatile procedures for adapting to natural changes. From agroforestry practices to the rebuilding of customary food frameworks, Native people group exhibit versatile methodologies that add to both environment flexibility and ecological equity.

Native people group frequently experience ecological prejudice, with the effects of natural debasement lopsidedly influencing the individuals who are minimized and need political power. The siting of dirtying enterprises, garbage removal destinations, and other ecological perils in or close to Native terrains reflects foundational examples of separation. This natural prejudice worsens existing social and monetary imbalances, prompting antagonistic wellbeing impacts, financial difficulties, and the disintegration of social practices.

Natural equity developments drove by Native people group effectively challenge ecological prejudice and look for change for verifiable and contemporary shameful acts. Grassroots getting sorted out, fights in court, and backing endeavors plan to consider businesses responsible for their natural effect, request government activity to address ecological bigotry, and guarantee that Native people group have a significant voice in choices that influence their current circumstance.

Native viewpoints on natural equity underscore the significance of diversity, perceiving that ecological issues are interconnected with more extensive battles for equity. The effects of ecological corruption meet with issues of racial unfairness, financial imbalance, and social eradication. Native drove developments frequently team up with other civil rights developments to address the main drivers of foundational treacheries and fabricate alliances for aggregate activity.

Innovation and development assume a double part in the convergence of Native points of view and ecological equity. While specific advancements add to natural corruption, others engage Native people group in observing and resolving ecological issues. From people group driven ecological checking undertakings to the utilization of satellite symbolism, innovation can give significant devices to social occasion information, considering polluters responsible, and supporting for strategy changes.

In any case, the sending of specific advances, like observation frameworks or extractive industry advancements, can happen in manners that adversely influence Native people group. Adjusting the advantages of innovation with the potential dangers requires cautious thought of force elements, social awareness, and the association of networks in dynamic cycles connected with mechanical mediations.

6.4 Intersectionality in the Fight for a Sustainable Future

Multifacetedness in the battle for a feasible future perceives the interconnected idea of social and ecological issues, understanding that different types of persecution and separation cross and compound, molding the encounters of people and networks. This approach recognizes that tending to ecological difficulties requires a comprehension of the mind boggling manners by which frameworks of force and honor work. From environmental change effects on inconsistent admittance to assets, multifacetedness features the requirement for comprehensive, far reaching arrangements that think about the variety of encounters and characters inside the more extensive setting of manageability.

Environmental change, quite possibly of the most squeezing natural test, excessively influences underestimated networks, enhancing existing social disparities. The effects of outrageous climate occasions, rising ocean levels, and interruptions to biological systems are felt most intensely by the individuals who are now helpless because of variables like race, class,

orientation, and geographic area. Low-pay networks, frequently made out of minorities, endure the worst part of environment related debacles, confronting difficulties like lacking foundation, restricted admittance to medical services, and deficient assets for recuperation.

The idea of natural equity, established in multifacetedness, addresses the inconsistent conveyance of ecological advantages and weights. Weak people group, generally minimized because of foundational bigotry and segregation, are bound to live in regions with elevated degrees of contamination, closeness to risky waste destinations, and defenselessness to environment related chances. The battle for ecological equity includes testing these fundamental disparities, upholding for strategies that focus on the prosperity of cutting edge networks, and guaranteeing that those most impacted have a voice in dynamic cycles.

Orientation converges with ecological issues in extraordinary ways, impacting how people insight and answer natural difficulties. Ladies, especially in underestimated networks, frequently bear an unbalanced weight in dealing with the effects of environmental change and ecological debasement. Conventional orientation jobs can restrict ladies' admittance to assets and dynamic power, making them more defenseless against the impacts of natural changes.

Simultaneously, ladies overall assume essential parts in economical practices, local area strength, and natural protection. Perceiving and enhancing the commitments of ladies in ecological stewardship is critical for cultivating a more comprehensive and viable way to deal with manageability. Orientation responsive strategies that address the particular requirements and difficulties looked by ladies add to a more fair and versatile reaction to ecological issues.

Native people group, with their special social viewpoints and profound association with the land, show the multifacetedness of natural and civil rights. Native people groups frequently wind up on the forefronts of ecological corruption, confronting the effects of asset extraction, land dispossession, and the interruption of conventional practices. The battle for Native freedoms and natural equity is interconnected, featuring the need to perceive and regard Native power, land privileges, and information frameworks.

Integrating Native points of view into the battle for a maintainable future includes focusing Native voices in dynamic cycles, recognizing the verifiable treacheries they have confronted, and supporting Native drove drives for protection and economical asset the board. This diverse methodology perceives the interconnectedness of natural and civil rights and underscores coordinated effort with Native people group as fundamental for building an additional supportable and simply future.

Race and nationality converge with ecological issues in manners that reflect verifiable and foundational examples of separation. Natural bigotry alludes to the act of putting ecological risks, like modern offices and harmful material locales, in or close to networks of variety.

This deliberate position propagates a pattern of natural unfairness, where minimized networks face more significant levels of contamination, unfavorable wellbeing impacts, and restricted admittance to assets for moderation and transformation.

The tradition of unfair practices, for example, redlining, adds to the convergence of natural weights in networks of variety. These verifiable treacheries highlight the requirement for strategies that address the main drivers of natural prejudice, challenge oppressive drafting rehearses, and guarantee that all networks have equivalent admittance to a sound climate. The battle against natural bigotry is fundamental to the more extensive development for ecological equity and a practical future.

Class crosses with ecological issues, forming people's and networks' capacity to adapt to and adjust to natural difficulties. Low-pay networks frequently miss the mark on monetary assets to alleviate the effects of environmental change or move notwithstanding natural catastrophes. Monetary inconsistencies add to inconsistent admittance to green spaces, clean energy, and other ecological conveniences.

The quest for financial development and benefit frequently compounds ecological corruption, prompting a situation where weak networks bear the natural weights while others receive the monetary rewards. Tending to the crossing point of class and ecological issues requires testing financial frameworks that focus on benefit over supportability, pushing for evenhanded monetary open doors, and guaranteeing that the change to a reasonable future doesn't lopsidedly trouble those with less assets.

Inability converges with ecological issues, impacting how people with incapacities experience and explore their surroundings. Ecological preparation and plan that consider openness and inclusivity are essential for guaranteeing that people with handicaps can completely take part in natural exercises and access regular spaces. In the midst of ecological calamities, people with handicaps might confront extra difficulties in clearing, cover access, and crisis reaction.

A multifaceted way to deal with incapacity and the climate perceives the variety of encounters inside the inability local area and under-scores the significance of comprehensive approaches and practices. This includes consolidating general plan standards, guaranteeing that natural drives think about the necessities of people with different capacities, and effectively remembering incapacitated voices for dynamic cycles connected with supportability.

The LGBTQ+ people group, as other underestimated gatherings, encounters multifacetedness with regards to ecological issues. Separation and social minimization meet with natural difficulties, molding how LGBTQ+ people access and experience the climate. For instance, the area of LGBTQ+ people group in metropolitan regions might open them to more significant levels of contamination, while segregation might restrict their admittance to protected and strong outside spaces.

A comprehensive and interconnected way to deal with ecological equity perceives the variety inside the LGBTQ+ people group and guarantees that natural arrangements and drives consider the interesting difficulties looked by LGBTQ+ people. Making protected and inviting green spaces, tending to separation in outside sporting spaces, and integrating LGBTQ+ viewpoints into ecological navigation add to an additional fair and economical future.

Ecological instruction converges with issues of access, portrayal, and inclusivity. Customary ecological schooling models have frequently ignored different points of view, sustaining a limited comprehension of natural issues and arrangements. An interconnected way to deal with ecological training stresses the significance of including voices from various foundations, societies, and networks to give a more exhaustive and exact comprehension of natural difficulties.

Guaranteeing that natural instruction is open to all people, paying little mind to financial status, race, orientation, or capacity, is critical for cultivating a more educated and drawn in populace. Comprehensive ecological training programs consider the different manners by which individuals experience and connect with the climate, empowering a more extensive scope of people to partake in the battle for a supportable future effectively.

The media assumes a huge part in molding public view of ecological issues and impacting strategy conversations. In any case, media portrayal frequently needs variety and may propagate generalizations or disregard the encounters of minimized networks. An interconnected way to deal with natural media portrayal includes intensifying the voices of those on the bleeding edges of ecological difficulties, testing one-sided stories, and featuring different points of view.

Utilizing different types of narrating, including narratives, writing, and workmanship, ecological equity developments influence media to refine the effects of natural debasement. Individual stories and local area stories furnish a strong method for interfacing with crowds on a profound level, encouraging compassion, and motivating activity. A multifaceted media approach perceives the significance of assorted narrating in building public mindfulness and backing for ecological equity.

Youth-drove developments, like Fridays for Future and the Dawn Development, have arisen as strong powers in the battle for a maintainable future. These developments, frequently drove by youthful activists, feature the intergenerational idea of ecological equity and the ethical basic to secure.

Chapter 7

Global Solidarity and Future Challenges

Worldwide fortitude is a basic idea that highlights the interconnectedness of the world and the requirement for cooperative endeavors to address shared difficulties. In a time set apart by mechanical progressions, monetary relationship, and natural worries, the call for worldwide fortitude resounds like never before.

One of the vital drivers of worldwide fortitude is the acknowledgment that no country or local area exists in seclusion. Occasions in a single corner of the world can have sweeping outcomes across borders, influencing economies, social orders, and biological systems. The Coronavirus pandemic clearly represented the fast spread of a worldwide emergency and the requirement for aggregate reactions. The infection, beginning in one area of the planet, immediately rose above public limits, underlining the significance of solidarity and collaboration.

Notwithstanding worldwide difficulties, fortitude turns into a useful asset for cultivating understanding and compassion among countries. It energizes the possibility that the prosperity of one is personally associated with the prosperity of all. This interconnectedness is clear in different parts of current life, from exchange and money to the climate and general wellbeing. The difficulties of the 21st hundred years, for example, environmental change, neediness, and general wellbeing emergencies, require cooperative endeavors that rise above public interests.

In the domain of financial aspects, the idea of worldwide fortitude difficulties conventional thoughts of rivalry and personal circumstance. It advocates for a more comprehensive and helpful way to deal with monetary turn of events, perceiving that economical advancement requires the interest and advantage, everything being equal. Worldwide exchange, for instance, is a sign of worldwide financial relationship, where nations trade labor and products to shared advantage.

Be that as it may, the advantages of globalization are not equally circulated, and inconsistencies continue among created and non-industrial countries. Worldwide fortitude, in this specific situation, suggests a pledge to tending to these imbalances, guaranteeing that the advantages of financial participation are shared impartially. Drives, for example, fair exchange and reasonable improvement objectives mean to make a more adjusted worldwide monetary framework that elevates the powerless and minimized.

Past financial contemplations, ecological difficulties highlight the earnest requirement for worldwide fortitude. Environmental change, deforestation, and biodiversity misfortune are issues that rise above public boundaries and require facilitated endeavors on a planetary scale. The strength of the planet is an aggregate liability, and moves made by one country can have expanding influences universally.

The Paris Understanding, endorsed by nations all over the planet, epitomizes a promise to aggregate activity to relieve environmental change. The understanding perceives that the effect of environmental change isn't bound to explicit locales and that a brought together reaction is fundamental. Worldwide fortitude in natural matters includes decreasing fossil fuel byproducts as well as supporting weak networks that endure the worst part of ecological corruption.

Essentially, general wellbeing crises, as shown by the Coronavirus pandemic, request worldwide fortitude as data sharing, asset allotment, and facilitated reaction endeavors. The capacity of an infection to cross boundaries quickly highlights the need of a cooperative way to deal with medical care. Antibodies, therapies, and clinical information should be shared universally to guarantee the prosperity of all.

In the domain of civil rights, worldwide fortitude difficulties imbued biases and predispositions that add to imbalance. Developments supporting for basic liberties, orientation equity, and racial equity underscore the interconnectedness of battles across various regions of the planet. Fortitude in this setting implies standing together against segregation and mistreatment, perceiving that equity and uniformity are widespread goals.

The approach of computerized correspondence and web-based entertainment has worked with the spread of data and thoughts, making a worldwide discussion on issues of social significance.

Developments like #BlackLivesMatter and #MeToo have risen above public limits, starting discussions and activities that reverberate around the world. Worldwide fortitude, in this sense, isn't simply a hypothetical idea however a lived experience formed by shared values and desires.

In any case, the way to worldwide fortitude isn't without challenges. Patriotism, protectionism, and international pressures can obstruct endeavors to encourage a feeling of shared liability. The quest for slender public interests to the detriment of worldwide collaboration sabotages the soul of fortitude and hampers progress on issues that require aggregate activity.

The dispersion of assets and power uneven characters likewise represents a test to worldwide fortitude. A few countries employ unbalanced impact in foreign relations, forming strategies and choices that influence the whole world. Addressing these uneven characters requires a guarantee to inclusivity and a reexamination of designs that propagate imbalance.

Moreover, the variety of societies, values, and political frameworks across the globe adds intricacy to the thought of worldwide fortitude. Spanning these distinctions requires discourse, understanding, and an eagerness to settle on some shared interest. Regard for social variety ought to be a fundamental piece of worldwide fortitude, perceiving that answers for worldwide provokes should be delicate to the interesting settings of various social orders.

Schooling assumes an essential part in developing a feeling of worldwide fortitude. By encouraging consciousness of worldwide issues, advancing multifaceted comprehension, and ingraining a feeling of shared liability, training can shape an age that embraces the standards of fortitude. In an interconnected world, an educated and sympathetic populace is fundamental for building spans across borders.

The job of worldwide associations is critical in propelling the reason for worldwide fortitude. Foundations like the Unified Countries, the World Wellbeing Association, and the Global Money related Asset act as stages for collaboration and coordination among countries. Reinforcing these organizations and guaranteeing their viability is fundamental for tending to worldwide difficulties altogether.

Despite future difficulties, like the effect of man-made reasoning, the ascent of new irresistible infections, and the possible results of environmental change, worldwide fortitude turns out to be significantly more basic. The fast speed of mechanical headways brings the two amazing open doors and dangers that rise above public limits. Moral contemplations, guidelines, and cooperative structures are important to explore the strange region of arising advancements.

The continuous discussion on the moral utilization of man-made brainpower epitomizes the requirement for a worldwide discourse and shared standards. As artificial intelligence turns out to be progressively incorporated into different parts of society, from medical care to back, laying

out standards that focus on common freedoms, protection, and decency is principal. Worldwide fortitude in the domain of innovation includes sharing ability as well as aggregately forming the moral establishments that administer its utilization.

The potential for new irresistible illnesses to arise and spread around the world features the significance of readiness and participation in general wellbeing. The examples gained from the Coronavirus pandemic highlight the requirement for a quick and facilitated worldwide reaction to arising wellbeing dangers. This incorporates the impartial dispersion of antibodies, sharing of clinical information, and cooperative examination endeavors.

Environmental change, with its expansive results, stays a considerable test that requires supported worldwide fortitude. The direness of moderating environmental change and adjusting to its effects requires striking and aggregate activity. Progressing to economical energy sources, safeguarding environments, and supporting weak networks are tries that request worldwide joint effort and responsibility.

In the domain of international relations, the potential for clashes and international pressures stays a danger to worldwide fortitude. The world has seen the outcomes of questions between countries, whether over domain, assets, or philosophical contrasts. Discretion, exchange, and compromise instruments are fundamental devices for encouraging comprehension and forestalling clashes that could sabotage worldwide participation.

The ascent of libertarian developments and the resurgence of patriotism in certain regions of the planet present difficulties to the soul of worldwide fortitude. These developments frequently focus on limited public interests over global collaboration and can add to a divided world request. Tending to the main drivers of these developments, like financial imbalances and social complaints, is pivotal for building a more comprehensive and helpful worldwide local area.

The job of authority in advancing worldwide fortitude couldn't possibly be more significant. Visionary pioneers who focus on cooperation, inclusivity, and the benefit of everyone can rouse a feeling of common perspective among countries. Initiative that rises above thin nationalistic interests and embraces a worldwide point of view is fundamental for exploring the perplexing difficulties of the 21st 100 years.

7.1 International Cooperation in Fighting Inequality

Worldwide collaboration in battling imbalance is a squeezing basic in a world described by interconnected economies, shared difficulties, and a developing consciousness of the worldwide elements of disparity. As monetary, social, and innovative powers shape the elements of our contemporary world, tending to imbalance requires cooperative endeavors that rise above public boundaries.

Financial imbalance, an unavoidable test, appears in different structures, including pay differences, abundance fixation, and inconsistent admittance to valuable open doors. The globalization of business sectors and the interconnected idea of economies imply that the results of financial imbalance are not restricted to public limits. The 2008 worldwide monetary emergency showed the way that financial shocks in a single region of the planet could have flowing impacts, highlighting the requirement for global collaboration to address the underlying drivers of imbalance.

At the core of financial imbalance lies the inconsistent conveyance of assets and potential open doors. Worldwide participation looks to amend these irregular characteristics by cultivating comprehensive financial development, guaranteeing fair exchange rehearses, and advancing manageable turn of events. Drives like the Unified Countries Feasible Improvement Objectives (SDGs) give a system to aggregate activity to kill destitution, lessen imbalance, and advance civil rights on a worldwide scale.

Exchange strategies assume a critical part in forming monetary elements and impacting the conveyance of abundance among countries. The idea of fair exchange underlines the significance of evenhanded exchanging connections that benefit all gatherings included, particularly powerless and minimized networks. Peaceful accords and establishments, like the World Exchange Association (WTO), plan to make a level battleground and forestall manipulative practices that add to worldwide monetary incongruities.

In any case, the adequacy of global participation in tending to financial disparity is dependent upon the responsibility of countries to carry out approaches that focus on inclusivity and civil rights. The ascent of protectionist measures and patriot opinions in a regions of the planet represents a test to the soul of participation, as nations might focus on their singular advantages over cooperative arrangements.

Social disparity, incorporating issues of training, medical care, and admittance to essential administrations, is another aspect that requests global collaboration. Differences in schooling add to a pattern of neediness and restricted open doors for some people, propagating social imbalance across ages. Cooperative endeavors to advance schooling as a principal right and to connect holes in admittance to quality training are fundamental for breaking this cycle.

Medical care imbalance is especially obvious even with worldwide wellbeing emergencies, like the Coronavirus pandemic. The pandemic uncovered the weaknesses in medical care frameworks overall and featured the requirement for an organized worldwide reaction. Admittance to immunizations, therapies, and clinical assets turned into a basic part of the worldwide work to control the spread of the infection, underlining the interconnected idea of general wellbeing.

Worldwide associations, like the World Wellbeing Association (WHO), assume a focal part in working with collaboration in the domain of worldwide wellbeing. The sharing of data, assets, and skill is pivotal for overseeing and forestalling the spread of irresistible illnesses. The pandemic highlighted the significance of an aggregate way to deal with general wellbeing crises, where no country can really battle a worldwide danger in detachment.

Additionally, tending to social disparity requires going up against issues of segregation, prohibition, and fundamental predispositions that sustain foul play. Developments upholding for orientation uniformity, racial equity, and LGBTQ+ privileges have picked up speed around the world, stressing the requirement for fortitude even with shared battles. Global participation in advancing basic liberties and battling segregation includes strategy structures as well as a social shift that encourages inclusivity and variety.

Mechanical headways, while offering phenomenal open doors, likewise add to new types of disparity. The advanced gap, where admittance to innovation and data is unevenly appropriated, compounds existing incongruities. Spanning the computerized hole requires worldwide cooperation to guarantee that the advantages of innovation are available to all, paying little heed to geological area or financial status.

In the domain of tax assessment, worldwide collaboration is urgent for forestalling tax avoidance and guaranteeing that partnerships contribute their reasonable portion to the social orders where they work. The capacity of worldwide enterprises to explore worldwide assessment frameworks and take advantage of escape clauses highlights the requirement for composed endeavors to lay out fair and straightforward expense approaches. Drives like the Association for Monetary Co-activity and Improvement's (OECD) Base Disintegration and Benefit Moving (BEPS) project plan to address these difficulties and make a more even-handed expense structure.

The ecological element of imbalance is a squeezing worry that rises above public boundaries. Environmental change, deforestation, and contamination lopsidedly influence weak networks, fueling existing social and monetary inconsistencies. Worldwide collaboration in natural preservation and maintainable advancement is basic for alleviating the unfavorable impacts of ecological corruption.

The Paris Understanding, a milestone worldwide accord, embodies aggregate endeavors to address environmental change on a worldwide scale. Countries meet up to set focuses for decreasing ozone harming substance outflows and to activate monetary assets to help environment versatile drives. Nonetheless, the adequacy of such arrangements depends on the responsibility of countries to execute and maintain their promises, as well as the acknowledgment that natural difficulties require cooperative, cross-line arrangements.

The job of worldwide monetary establishments, like the Global Financial Asset (IMF) and the World Bank, is critical in tending to worldwide monetary disparities. These establishments assume a critical part in giving monetary help, specialized mastery, and strategy direction to countries confronting financial difficulties. Notwithstanding, the circumstances appended to credits and help bundles should focus on comprehensive and supportable turn of events, guaranteeing that the advantages arrive at the more extensive populace.

The Coronavirus pandemic brought to the very front the significance of worldwide collaboration in the midst of emergency. The quick spread of the infection and its expansive financial and social outcomes highlighted the interconnectedness of the worldwide local area. Immunization circulation, financial boost bundles, and obligation alleviation drives became central places of worldwide joint effort, featuring the need of fortitude in exploring shared difficulties.

Difficulties to worldwide collaboration in battling disparity continue, established in issues of force elements, international strains, and varying public interests. The impact of major monetary powers in forming worldwide arrangements can in some cases lead to uneven characters that frustrate endeavors to address disparity. Spanning these holes requires political endeavors, exchange, and a guarantee to making a more comprehensive and delegate worldwide request.

International pressures and clashes can hinder the soul of global participation, redirecting assets and consideration from cooperative endeavors to battle disparity. Discretion, compromise components, and a common obligation to harmony are fundamental for cultivating a climate helpful for tending to the main drivers of disparity.

The job of common society and non-legislative associations (NGOs) is instrumental in considering states and global organizations responsible for their responsibilities to battling imbalance. Grassroots developments, backing efforts, and local area based drives add to bringing issues to light and forcing leaders to focus on comprehensive arrangements.

7.2 Emerging Social Justice Movements

Arising civil rights developments are reshaping the worldwide scene, testing existing power structures, and supporting for an additional comprehensive and evenhanded world. These developments, frequently conceived out of grassroots activism and powered by computerized network, address a horde of issues going from racial and orientation fairness to natural equity. Their effect reaches out past public boundaries, encouraging a feeling of shared battle and rousing aggregate activity on a worldwide scale.

The People of color Matter (BLM) development has been a strong power in featuring foundational prejudice and police ruthlessness. Starting in the US, BLM picked up global speed, reverberating with individuals overall who had comparable worries about racial shamefulness. The development underlines the need to address well established imbalances, challenge unfair practices, and advance responsibility in policing.

Online entertainment stages play had a crucial impact in enhancing the voices of these developments, giving a space to activists to share data, sort out occasions, and prepare support. Hashtags, for example, #BlackLivesMatter and #SayHerName have become images of fortitude, rising above topographical limits and cultivating a worldwide discussion about racial treachery.

Likewise, the Me Too development has started a worldwide retribution with lewd behavior and attack. What started as a hashtag via web-based entertainment developed into a strong development that rises above public boundaries, as survivors from different nations shared their encounters and requested responsibility. The Me Too development highlights the commonness of orientation based viciousness and promoters for social and foundational changes to establish more secure conditions for all.

Ecological equity developments, moved by the earnest need to address environmental change, feature the unbalanced effect of natural corruption on minimized networks. Native people groups, networks of variety, and those with lower financial status frequently endure the worst part of ecological dangers and environment related calamities. The call for natural equity advocates for fair and comprehensive strategies that think about the interconnection of social and ecological issues.

Greta Thunberg, a Swedish teen dissident, arose as a noticeable figure in the worldwide youth-drove environment development. The Fridays for Future development, started by Thunberg, saw youngsters all over the planet taking part in strikes and fights to request activity on environmental change. The development underscores the interconnectedness of natural issues and civil rights, pushing for approaches that focus on maintainability and address the underlying drivers of environmental change.

The LGBTQ+ privileges development has taken huge steps in supporting for the freedoms and nobility of people no matter what their sexual direction or orientation character. While progress has been made in a few nations, challenges persevere worldwide. Activists and associations work to battle separation, advance inclusivity, and challenge harsh regulations that condemn or underestimate LGBTQ+ people. The development means to make an existence where everybody can reside really and liberated from oppression.

These civil rights developments share consistent ideas - a guarantee to destroying harsh frameworks, enhancing underestimated voices, and cultivating a feeling of worldwide fortitude. The utilization of computerized stages for coordinating and backing has been a distinct advantage, empowering developments to rise above geological limits and interface with similar people and gatherings around the world.

The idea of diversity, advocated by researcher Kimberlé Crenshaw, is vital to numerous civil rights developments. It perceives that people experience various meeting types of persecution and segregation in light of elements like race, orientation, sexuality, and class. Multifacetedness energizes a more nuanced comprehension of social issues and stresses the requirement for comprehensive arrangements that address the intricacy of people's lived encounters.

The effect of civil rights developments reaches out to strategy changes, social moves, and expanded mindfulness. Following fights against racial foul play, there has been a restored center around police change, the evacuation of images related with expansionism and prejudice, and endeavors to address fundamental disparities in different areas. The impact of these developments isn't bound to explicit locales; their requests for equity and uniformity reverberate internationally, rousing discussions and activities across borders.

In any case, civil rights developments additionally face difficulties and pushback. Protection from change, dug in power structures, and the weaponization of deception present huge impediments. Activists might confront dangers, provocation, and brutality as they defy strong interests and challenge instilled biases. Exploring these difficulties requires flexibility, vital reasoning, and a supported obligation to the standards of equity and balance.

The job of partners in civil rights developments is essential. Partners are people or gatherings who support a reason regardless of whether they straightforwardly experience the mistreatment being referred to. The People of color Matter development, for example, acquired help from individuals of different racial and ethnic foundations who perceived the significance of tending to racial disparity. Fortitude among different gatherings reinforces developments, making a more considerable power for change.

Global fortitude has turned into a sign of civil rights developments, as activists perceive the interconnectedness of battles across borders. The battle against foul play isn't restricted to explicit countries; rather, an aggregate undertaking requires cooperation and backing from people and gatherings all over the planet. Worldwide issues, for example, environmental change and common freedoms infringement request global participation and a unified front against fundamental treacheries.

The language of civil rights has developed to include individual freedoms as well as aggregate prosperity. Developments progressively stress the interconnectedness of different battles, upholding for an all encompassing way to deal with equity that tends to the main drivers of disparity. The possibility that equity is inseparable highlights the need to think about the more extensive effect of strategies and practices on whole networks and social orders.

Schooling assumes a crucial part in forming the story and encouraging compassion and understanding. Civil rights developments frequently include instructive drives that challenge one-sided educational plans, advance decisive reasoning, and enhance different voices. By cultivating a consciousness of social issues, developments expect to make a more educated and drawn in populace that effectively partakes chasing equity.

The job of workmanship and culture in civil rights developments couldn't possibly be more significant. Music, visual expressions, writing, and different types of innovative articulation act as integral assets for passing on messages, motivating compassion, and testing cultural standards. Craftsmen add to the account of developments, encapsulating obstruction and strength in their work. Social moves frequently go before or go with more extensive social and political change.

Civil rights developments likewise draw in with legitimate and institutional systems to achieve change. Promotion for strategy changes, testing oppressive regulations, and considering foundations responsible are fundamental parts of numerous developments. The fights in court battled by activists add to the foundation of points of reference that can shape future regulation and safeguard the privileges of minimized networks.

The developing idea of civil rights developments mirrors a developing consciousness of the interconnected difficulties confronting humankind. Developments are not generally bound to explicit issues or geographic areas; they perceive the requirement for a far reaching and interconnected way to deal with equity. Activists progressively team up across developments, perceiving that the battle against mistreatment is a common undertaking that requires aggregate activity.

7.3 Challenges and Opportunities in the Pursuit of Equality

The quest for balance is a central part of basic freedoms and civil rights, planning to guarantee that all people have equivalent open doors, admittance to assets, and the capacity to take part completely in the public eye. While progress has been made in different regions, critical difficulties continue, and the excursion toward uniformity is set apart by intricacies and continuous battles. All the while, the quest for balance presents potential open doors for groundbreaking change, imaginative arrangements, and the production of an additional comprehensive and simply world.

One of the focal difficulties in accomplishing uniformity is the steadiness of foundational separation and underlying imbalances. These imbalances are profoundly imbued in friendly, financial, and political frameworks, propagating abberations in light of variables like race, orientation, financial status, and different types of character. Defeating these well established structures requires tending to individual demonstrations of separation as well as destroying the foundational boundaries that propagate imbalance.

Authentic traditions of segregation, for example, organized prejudice and expansionism, keep on molding contemporary difficulties chasing after fairness. The verifiable disappointment of specific gatherings has long haul results, affecting admittance to instruction, financial open doors, and political portrayal. Recognizing and changing these verifiable treacheries is fundamental for making an establishment whereupon genuine uniformity can be fabricated.

Financial imbalance stays a tireless and multi-layered challenge that converges with different components of character. Variations in pay and abundance circulation, frequently exacerbated by factors like orientation and race, add to inconsistent admittance to open doors and assets. The grouping of abundance in the possession of a couple can sustain patterns of destitution and breaking point social portability. Tending to monetary imbalance requires redistributive strategies as well as a reexamination of the designs that sustain abundance variations.

Schooling assumes a critical part in forming future open doors and results, yet instructive disparity stays a huge obstacle chasing fairness. Abberations in instructive assets, nature of schools, and admittance to advanced education add to inconsistent life possibilities. Kids from underestimated networks might confront fundamental hindrances that limit their instructive achievement, sustaining patterns of impediment. Making a fair school system includes tending to asset incongruities, taking out unfair practices, and encouraging a comprehensive learning climate.

In the working environment, orientation and racial variations endure, reflecting more extensive cultural disparities. The orientation pay hole, underrepresentation of ladies and minorities in administrative roles, and working environment segregation ruin progress toward balance. Advancing variety and incorporation, carrying out straightforward compensation rehearses, and testing orientation and racial inclinations are urgent strides toward making work environments that mirror the standards of uniformity.

Segregation in view of orientation personality and sexual direction stays a critical test to accomplishing correspondence. LGBTQ+ people might confront segregation in different parts of life, including business, training, and admittance to medical care. Legitimate acknowledgment and assurance of LGBTQ+ privileges, alongside social moves that challenge marks of disgrace and predispositions, are fundamental for cultivating a comprehensive society where all people can reside genuinely and liberated from segregation.

Natural equity is an arising aspect of the quest for uniformity. Minimized people group frequently bear the unbalanced weight of ecological risks, contamination, and the effects of environmental change. Guaranteeing that ecological arrangements focus on the prosperity of weak populaces and address the diversity of natural and social issues is pivotal for propelling fairness even with worldwide natural difficulties.

Admittance to medical care is a crucial part of prosperity, yet well-being differences endure, excessively influencing underestimated networks. Factors, for example, financial status, race, and geographic area can affect admittance to quality medical care administrations. Accomplishing wellbeing value includes tending to the social determinants of wellbeing, killing obstructions to medical care access, and guaranteeing that medical services approaches focus on the requirements, everything being equal, paying little mind to personality or foundation.

Political portrayal is a vital part of guaranteeing that different voices are heard and that dynamic cycles are comprehensive. Be that as it may, ladies, minorities, and other underestimated bunches are frequently underrepresented in political positions of authority. Advancing comprehensive political frameworks, executing electing changes, and addressing obstructions to political cooperation are crucial stages toward accomplishing equity in administration and strategy making.

While challenges proliferate, the quest for equity additionally presents open doors for extraordinary change and positive effect. Propels in innovation and correspondence, for instance, give new roads to arranging and assembling developments for civil rights. Web-based entertainment stages intensify minimized voices, work with worldwide fortitude, and take into consideration the fast spread of data that challenges abusive accounts.

Developments in schooling, like web based learning stages and open instructive assets, can possibly democratize admittance to information and extension instructive holes. These instruments can enable people from different foundations to obtain abilities and information, opening new open doors for individual and expert development.

Corporate and hierarchical responsibilities to variety, value, and consideration address a positive change in tending to work environment disparity. Organizations perceiving the worth of different viewpoints are executing strategies and drives to advance comprehensive societies, dispense with inclinations, and guarantee equivalent open doors for professional success.

Legitimate and strategy progressions are basic chasing correspondence. Official changes that address oppressive practices, safeguard underestimated gatherings, and elevate inclusivity add to making an all the more society. Worldwide basic freedoms systems give an establishment to supporting uniformity on a worldwide scale, underscoring the common obligation of countries to maintain the standards of equity and decency.

Support and activism keep on being useful assets chasing balance. Grassroots developments, drove by people and networks straightforwardly impacted by disparity, have the ability to drive social and political change.

The worldwide idea of numerous contemporary difficulties takes into account the development of transnational coalitions and organizations, enhancing the effect of backing endeavors.

Schooling, as an impetus for social change, assumes a critical part in advancing correspondence. Educational programs that reflect assorted points of view, comprehensive showing rehearses, and instructive strategies that address foundational hindrances add to establishing an even-handed learning climate. Instruction bestows information as well as shapes mentalities and values, making it an incredible asset for testing generalizations and cultivating compassion.

Social portrayals and stories are instrumental in forming cultural perspectives toward uniformity. Media, writing, and human expressions have the ability to challenge generalizations, feature different encounters, and add to a more comprehensive social scene. Supporting and advancing different voices in media and artistic expressions can prompt a more exact and nuanced portrayal of the intricacies of human encounters.

Local area commitment and participatory methodologies are fundamental for guaranteeing that drives pointed toward accomplishing fairness are educated by the necessities and viewpoints regarding the networks they look to serve. Including underestimated bunches in dynamic cycles, paying attention to their encounters, and esteeming their feedback are critical for making supportable and powerful arrangements.

Worldwide collaboration is essential in addressing worldwide difficulties to correspondence. Shared issues, for example, environmental change, financial disparity, and the relocation of populaces, require cooperative endeavors on a worldwide scale. Arrangements, deals, and drives that elevate global collaboration add to an existence where countries cooperate to address shared difficulties and maintain the standards of equity and correspondence.

7.4 The Role of Individuals in Driving Lasting Change

The job of people in driving enduring change is a major part of cultural advancement and change. Over the entire course of time, people play played critical parts in molding developments, testing standards, and upholding for positive change. Whether through demonstrations of fortitude, creative reasoning, or grassroots endeavors, people have the ability to impact and drive enduring change in different spaces, including governmental issues, civil rights, ecological manageability, and innovation.

Political change frequently starts with people who are propelled to rock the boat and work towards an all the more and fair society. Visionary pioneers, like Mahatma Gandhi, Nelson Mandela, and Martin Luther Ruler Jr., embody the groundbreaking effect of individual organization in driving political change.

These figures, through their obligation to peaceful opposition and their capacity to prepare networks, added to critical social and political movements that rose above public limits.

As of late, the job of people in political change has been featured by grassroots developments and social activism. Developments like Involve Money Road, the Bedouin Spring, and the worldwide environment strikes have exhibited the influence of aggregate activity started by people. Virtual entertainment stages, giving phenomenal network, have permitted people to sort out and enhance their voices, prompting developments that request fundamental change and challenge laid out power structures.

People likewise assume a critical part in propelling civil rights and value. Activists and supporters who champion the privileges of minimized networks add to moving cultural mentalities and arrangements. Figures like Malala Yousafzai, upholding for young ladies' schooling, and Tarana Burke, the organizer behind the #MeToo development, have become images of flexibility and impetuses for social change. Their endeavors feature the extraordinary capability of people in resolving issues of separation, disparity, and foul play.

In the domain of ecological supportability, people can drive change through their decisions, ways of behaving, and backing. The idea of "ecological citizenship" underscores the obligations people have in adding to an economical future. Endeavors like decreasing carbon impressions, taking on eco-accommodating practices, and pushing for natural strategies add to an aggregate effect on biological difficulties. The activities of ecological activists, as Greta Thunberg, highlight the impact people can have in bringing issues to light and compelling states and companies to address environmental change.

Mechanical progressions have given people new apparatuses to drive change in uncommon ways. The democratization of data through the web and virtual entertainment permits people to get to information, share thoughts, and associate with similar people universally. Stages like Kickstarter and GoFundMe engage people to raise money for purposes they put stock in, encouraging another period of grassroots drives and local area driven projects.

In the domain of innovation, people likewise add to advancement and change through business and logical revelation. Trend-setters like Steve Occupations, Elon Musk, and Marie Curie have changed enterprises as well as molded the manner in which society capabilities. The improvement of new innovations, from environmentally friendly power answers for clinical forward leaps, frequently begins from the endeavors of people who imagine a superior future and devote their abilities and assets to making it a reality.

The job of people in driving enduring change reaches out to the social and creative circle. Journalists, specialists, and artists frequently act as social powerhouses, testing standards and forming public talk. Scholarly works like Harriet Beecher Stowe's "Uncle Tom's Lodge" and

George Orwell's "1984" have affected cultural discernments and started discussions about civil rights and political situation. Also, performers and specialists add to social developments, utilizing their foundation to resolve issues like prejudice, disparity, and basic liberties.

Schooling, as a device for enabling people, assumes a fundamental part in driving enduring change. Instructors, researchers, and instructive organizations add to molding viewpoints, encouraging decisive reasoning, and imparting upsides of compassion and social obligation. People who commit themselves to training, whether in formal or casual environments, add to building a general public that values information, inclusivity, and the quest for equity.

The force of narrating can't be undervalued in that frame of mind of driving enduring change. Accounts can shape discernments, challenge generalizations, and move activity. People who share their own accounts, whether through diaries, narratives, or virtual entertainment, add to building sympathy and understanding. Developments, for example, the LGBTQ+ freedoms development have been altogether moved by people who gallantly shared their accounts, adding to cultural changes in mentalities and approaches.

Nonetheless, the way to driving enduring change isn't without challenges. People frequently face obstruction, backfire, and impediments as they challenge laid out standards and power structures. The anxiety toward backlash, social segregation, or individual gamble can stop people from making intense moves. Defeating these difficulties requires versatility, cooperation, and the help of networks that share a typical vision of positive change.

The job of people in driving enduring change is interconnected with the idea of authority. Successful pioneers motivate, prepare, and guide others toward a common vision of a superior future. Administration isn't bound to formal positions; people at any degree of society can show authority characteristics by stepping up to the plate, exhibiting trustworthiness, and affecting positive change inside their effective reaches.

Cooperation and aggregate activity upgrade the effect of individual endeavors. Developments for change frequently pick up speed when people meet up to shape partnerships, share assets, and intensify their voices. The force of aggregate activity is obvious in developments like the social liberties development, women's activist developments, and contemporary developments for racial equity, where various people joined for a typical reason have driven significant cultural changes.

The job of people in driving enduring change isn't restricted to explicit segment gatherings or financial situations with. Change-producers can rise up out of any foundation, and the variety of viewpoints improves the texture of social developments. Perceiving and esteeming the commitments of people from various different backgrounds is fundamental for making comprehensive and feasible change.

Compassion and a profound comprehension of the encounters of others are pivotal for compelling change-production. People who relate to the battles of underestimated networks, perceive their honor, and effectively work to destroy severe designs add to making an all the more and fair society. Sympathy cultivates fortitude and urges people to involve their organization in the assistance of more extensive social objectives.

The job of people in driving enduring change isn't restricted to explicit issues or geological limits. Worldwide difficulties, for example, environmental change, pandemics, and basic liberties infringement, require global cooperation and the aggregate endeavors of people around the world. Developments with worldwide reach, worked with by computerized network, feature the interconnectedness of cultural issues and the requirement for a common obligation to positive change.

Schooling and mindfulness building are fundamental parts of people driving enduring change. Understanding the main drivers of cultural issues, basically inspecting laid out standards, and cultivating a feeling of obligation toward aggregate prosperity add to educated and effective change-production. Schooling enables people to address, challenge, and imagine elective prospects.

All in all, the job of people in driving enduring change is diverse, enveloping political activism, civil rights promotion, ecological steward-ship, mechanical development, imaginative articulation, schooling, and that's only the tip of the iceberg. People who rock the boat, rouse aggregate activity, and add to a dream of a superior world are the main impetus behind cultural advancement. While difficulties and hindrances exist, the extraordinary capability of people to shape the course of history and construct an all the more, comprehensive, and feasible future is a demonstration of the getting through force of human organization.

People, through their organization and aggregate endeavors, assume a urgent part in driving enduring change across different spaces, includ-ing governmental issues, civil rights, ecological manageability, innova-tion, and culture. The extraordinary effect of people is clear from the beginning of time and in contemporary developments that rock the boat, advocate for equity, and move positive cultural movements.

Political change frequently depends on the activities of people who question laid out standards and work toward an all the more and im-partial society. Mahatma Gandhi, with his way of thinking of peaceful obstruction, prepared masses in India to challenge English provincial rule. His obligation to common noncompliance and the standards of Satyagraha turned into a model for ensuing developments around the world, impacting pioneers like Martin Luther Ruler Jr. in the US and Nelson Mandela in South Africa.

Nelson Mandela, a notorious figure in the battle against politically-sanctioned racial segregation, burned through 27 years in jail for his enemy of politically-sanctioned racial segregation exercises. His versa-tility, obligation to compromise, and visionary initiative assumed a urgent part in South Africa's progress to a post-politically-sanctioned racial segregation time. Mandela's excursion from detainee to president represents the getting through influence people can have on molding political scenes and destroying harsh frameworks.

In the contemporary time, grassroots developments driven by people utilizing computerized stages have become strong specialists of political change. The Bedouin Spring, a progression of fights across the Center East and North Africa, was energized by people utilizing virtual entertainment to sort out and enhance their voices. These developments, however different in their causes and results, highlight the limit of people to assemble and challenge dictator systems.

Civil rights developments, established in the endeavors of people upholding for equity and value, have been instrumental in reshaping cultural standards. The #BlackLivesMatter development arose in light of police viciousness and fundamental bigotry, getting some decent forward movement through the activism of people focused on tending to racial shamefulness. The development epitomizes the power of individual voices in bringing issues to light, impacting public talk, and requesting foundational change.

Malala Yousafzai, a youthful backer for young ladies' schooling, endure a death endeavor by the Taliban and proceeded to turn into a worldwide image of versatility and activism. Malala's obligation to training for all, particularly young ladies in areas impacted by struggle, features the extraordinary force of people, even despite misfortune.

Tarana Burke, the pioneer behind the #MeToo development, made a stage for overcomers of lewd behavior and attack to share their encounters. The development picked up speed universally, with people from different foundations approaching to reveal insight into unavoidable issues of orientation based viciousness. Burke's promotion represents the way in which people can make developments that challenge dug in cultural standards and backer for social and foundational change.

Natural maintainability, a basic worldwide issue, has seen people assuming a huge part in driving change. Greta Thunberg, a Swedish high school extremist, started the Fridays for Future development, rousing understudies overall to take part in strikes requesting earnest activity on environmental change. Thunberg's capacity to excite a worldwide youth development exhibits the effect of individual responsibility on bringing issues to light and requesting responsibility from pioneers.

People additionally add to mechanical development, molding the manner in which society works and tending to squeezing difficulties. Business visionaries like Steve Occupations, through the formation of Mac, upset the innovation and correspondence scene. Elon Musk's endeavors, including Tesla and SpaceX, exhibit how people can drive development in supportable energy and space investigation.

Marie Curie, a spearheading researcher, made momentous commitments to the fields of material science and science, turning into the main lady to win a Nobel Prize and the main individual to win Nobel Prizes in two different logical fields. Curie's heritage shows how people, through their logical undertakings, can reshape how we might interpret the world and add to headways that benefit mankind.

In the domain of innovation, people add to extraordinary change through business as well as through logical disclosure and examination. Advancements in fields like man-made brainpower, sustainable power, and biotechnology frequently originate from the endeavors of people who commit their abilities and mastery to tending to complex difficulties.

The democratization of data worked with by the web has enabled people to drive grassroots drives and local area driven projects. Crowdfunding stages like Kickstarter and GoFundMe permit people to raise assets for purposes they have confidence in, going from civil rights drives to local area advancement projects. These stages democratize the method involved with subsidizing, empowering people to activate support for their thoughts and ventures.

The job of people in molding social accounts and testing cultural standards is clear in the fields of writing, craftsmanship, and music. Authors, specialists, and performers frequently act as social powerhouses, utilizing their foundation to address laid out standards and promoter for social change.

Harriet Beecher Stowe's book "Uncle Tom's Lodge" assumed a critical part in forming popular assessment against subjection in the US. The book, which depicted the unforgiving real factors of subjugation, added to the abolitionist development and featured the force of narrating in affecting cultural discernments.

George Orwell's "1984" stays an original work that scrutinizes tyranny and observation, filling in as a wake up call about the risks of uncontrolled power. Scholarly works like Orwell's add to a more extensive social discussion about political frameworks, individual opportunities, and cultural qualities.

Performers and craftsmen, through their imaginative articulations, have been persuasive in driving cultural change. The social equality development in the US, drove by figures like Martin Luther Ruler Jr., was joined by strong melodies that became songs of devotion of the development. Craftsmen like Bounce Dylan and Nina Simone utilized their music to challenge foul play and backer for social liberties.

In the contemporary time, the LGBTQ+ freedoms development has been essentially pushed by people who bravely shared their accounts. The individual stories of people inside the LGBTQ+ people group, enhanced through web-based entertainment and creative articulations, have added to changing cultural perspectives and pushing for legitimate acknowledgment and insurances.

Schooling, as a device for strengthening and cultural change, depends on the devotion of people focused on cultivating decisive reasoning, inclusivity, and social obligation. Educators, researchers, and instructive establishments add to molding points of view, encouraging compassion, and imparting values that advance positive cultural change.

The force of narrating, worked with by people who share their own stories, has been instrumental in driving discussions around issues like psychological wellness, variety, and consideration. Stages like TED Talks give people the chance to share their encounters and bits of knowledge, cultivating a worldwide discourse on points that influence people and networks.

Local area commitment and participatory methodologies improve the effect of individual endeavors in driving enduring change. Drives drove by people who work cooperatively with networks, pay attention to assorted points of view, and focus on inclusivity are bound to make economical and significant changes.

Authority, showed by people who motivate, prepare, and guide others toward a common vision, is a basic component in driving enduring change. Successful pioneers, whether in conventional positions or grassroots developments, show characteristics like sympathy, trustworthiness, and a promise to equity. Authority isn't bound to explicit jobs; people at any degree of society can show administration characteristics by stepping up and affecting positive change inside their effective reaches.

Cooperation and aggregate activity enhance the effect of individual endeavors. Developments for change frequently pick up speed when people meet up to frame unions, share assets, and enhance their voices. The force of aggregate activity is clear in developments like the social equality development, women's activist developments, and contemporary developments for racial equity, where different people joined for a typical reason have driven significant cultural changes.

The job of people in driving enduring change isn't restricted to explicit segment gatherings or financial situations with. Change-creators can rise out of any foundation, and the variety of points of view advances the texture of social developments.

Perceiving and esteeming the commitments of people from various different backgrounds is fundamental for making comprehensive and supportable change.

Sympathy, a profound comprehension of the encounters of others, is essential for powerful change-production. People who understand the battles of minimized networks, perceive their honor, and effectively work to destroy harsh designs add to making an all the more and impartial society. Sympathy cultivates fortitude and urges people to involve their organization in the help of more extensive social objectives.

9 783061 401221